STRAIGHT TALK
TO LEADERS

What we wish we had
known when we started

Books in This Series

When God Seems Silent
Straight Talk To Leaders
Battle Cry for Your Marriage

More books in this series coming soon

Finding Freedom and Staying Free!
Experiencing the Supernatural

The TIME Is NOW! Series

STRAIGHT TALK TO LEADERS

What we wish we had known when we started

Larry Kreider, Sam Smucker,
Barry Wissler and Lester Zimmerman

House To House Publications
Lititz, Pennsylvania USA
www.h2hp.com

Straight Talk to Leaders
What we wish we had known when we started
by Larry Kreider, Sam Smucker, Barry Wissler
and Lester Zimmerman

Copyright © 2015 Larry Kreider, Sam Smucker, Barry Wissler
and Lester Zimmerman

Published by
House to House Publications
11 Toll Gate Road, Lititz, PA 17543 USA
Telephone: 800.848.5892
www.h2hp.com

ISBN 10: 0990429350
ISBN 13: 978-0-9904293-5-7

CONTENTS

How to Use This Resource

Personal study

Read from start to finish and receive personal revelation. Learn spiritual truths to help yourself and others.

- Each reading includes questions for personal reflection and room to journal at the end of the book.
- Each chapter has a key verse to memorize.

Daily devotional

Eight weeks of daily readings with corresponding questions for personal reflection and journaling.

- Each chapter is divided into seven sections for weekly use.
- Each day includes reflection questions and space to journal.

Mentoring relationship

Questions can be answered and life applications discussed when this book is used as a one-on-one discipling/mentoring tool.

- A spiritual mentor can easily take a person they are mentoring through these short Bible study lessons and use the reflection questions for dialogue about what is learned.
- Study each day's entry or an entire chapter at a time.

Small group study

Study in a small group setting or in a class or Bible study group.

- The teacher teaches the material using the outline provided at the end of the book. Everyone in the group reads the chapter and discusses the questions together.

Introduction

Sam Smucker, Barry Wissler, Lester Zimmerman and I (Larry Kreider) grew up as farm boys in Lancaster and Lebanon Counties in south-central Pennsylvania. Each of us received God's call between the late 1970s and early 1980s to lead new churches. Each of us have been humbled and blessed as the churches we have led continue to grow and birth new churches and ministries, which serve multiplied thousands of believers and communities in more than a hundred nations.

Sam, Barry, Lester and I have been friends for more than 35 years. We have taught in each other's leadership schools and each of us train leaders throughout the world. I know these men well. Many times I have witnessed them sharing their own life stories, which provide amazing leadership insights to younger leaders.

Recently I asked these three friends if they would co-write a book with me about leadership. Without hesitation, each immediately responded affirmatively and promised to share fourteen key leadership principles that they learned during the past forty years. The book you hold in your hands is the finished product compiling 56 key leadership lessons.

In all honesty, we wish we could have read a book like this when we were younger. It would have saved us from learning the hard way. Our prayer is that this book will help you avoid many pitfalls in your journey to healthy leadership.

Although much of the focus in this book is on church leadership, the principles also apply to leadership in other arenas including businesses, organizations, and community positions.

As a team of writers, we wanted to make this book as user friendly as possible. You can read this book from cover to cover. Or you can study one section each day for the next two months. Or you may form a group with others who want to learn about leadership and study one chapter a week for eight weeks. Discussion questions for each chapter are included to help you digest and apply what you are learning.

God bless you as you read and apply these leadership insights. Our desire is to help you become the healthy leader our God has called you to be.

— Larry Kreider, Sam Smucker, Barry Wissler
and Lester Zimmerman

CHAPTER 1

Vision, Accountability and Building Healthy Teams

Sam Smucker

Keep Your Eyes on the Fencepost

"But Jesus told him, 'Anyone who puts a hand to the plow and then looks back is not fit for the Kingdom of God'" (Luke 9:62 NLT).

When I was about 12 years old, my father said one morning, "Today I am going to teach you how to plow."

I was raised in an Amish family, which meant we did our farm work with mules. I had worked with mules since I was five years old, but this was different. This meant my father trusted me enough to teach me how to do the most important task in the field work.

I was both excited and scared as we bridled and harnessed our four mules named Dick, Pete, Jack and Jewel. When we got to the starting point, the field looked so big to me. My father said, "It is very important to start with a straight furrow the first time through the field. If the first furrow is not straight, it will affect the whole field. Do you see that fencepost at the end of the field?"

> Do not look down or look to the right or to the left. . . Do not look back.

I said, "Yes I see it."

He said, "Keep your eyes on that fencepost until you get to the other end. Do not look down or look to the right or to the left. Do not look at the mules. Do not look back. Do not take your eyes off of the fencepost until you get to the other end."

I gave the mules the signal to begin. I did exactly what my Dad told me to do by keeping my eyes on the fencepost until I got to the other end. When I reached the end, I looked back and the furrow was perfectly straight.

Later in life when I answered the calling that God had for me, I realized the spiritual correlation of that fencepost lesson. There are many distractions in life and ministry. Many times throughout 38 years of pastoring a church I recalled my father's admonition to keep my eyes fixed ahead, not looking to the right or left. When a person is called to leadership, vision becomes a very important part of leading. Proverbs 29:18 says, "Where there is no vision, the people perish." One of the responsibilities of a leader is to keep the vision in front of the people. When the vision is clear and easy to follow much can be accomplished for the Kingdom of God. So the vision must be talked about on an ongoing basis.

Throughout years of pastoring, I have learned whenever I get tired of promoting the vision is when most of the hearers only begin to understand

REFLECTION
Name things that distract you from your goal.

it. Therefore promoting vision is ongoing and should never stop. The last church facility we built took us ten years from planning until the time we moved in. Sometimes it became difficult to keep the vision fresh and clear. Those are the times a leader must dig deep to hear from the Holy Spirit for inspiration to share the vision one more time.

Accountability and Relationship

DAY 2

"Dear brothers and sisters, if another believer is overcome by some sin, you who are godly should gently and humbly help that person back onto the right path. And be careful not to fall into the same temptation yourself. Share each other's burdens, and in this way obey the law of Christ. If you think you are too important to help someone, you are only fooling yourself. You are not that important" (Galatians 6:1-3 NLT).

"So encourage each other and build each other up, just as you are already doing" (1 Thessalonians 5:11).

Leaders need a solid wall of protection around them. Sherlyn and I have always been blessed to have close friends and peers with whom we share our lives and are accountable. We have intentionally given permission for them to speak into our lives. We also enjoy fun and relaxation with them.

> Even though we take days off, we are never really off duty.

I encourage each ministry couple to have similar friends in their lives. Too many leader couples have no close friends to share their lives with and consequently feel alone. The enemy can use this to bring discouragement and temptation. If the wrong situation presents itself, the leader may not have the strength to resist the temptation.

You may say we don't have anyone with whom to have this kind of relationship. I encourage you to ask the Lord to bring these kinds of relationships into your life. It could be a couple in your area or even someone not in your town.

Several years before Sherlyn and I answered the call to ministry, we lost our sixteen-month-old son in a traffic accident. Our son, Christopher, had wandered on to the road and was hit by a vehicle. He died because of the accident. This, of course, was a very difficult time for us to face and walk through. At that time we were part of a group of people who had started a Bible study in Southern Lancaster County. When we had the viewing for our son, many came to extend their condolences to us. One couple came through the viewing line. The moment I looked at the husband there was a deep connection; we embraced and wept. Before that time, I did not know this man very well. From that moment to now—forty one years later—we have been closest friends. This couple became pastors after that Bible study grew into a church. They have served as our pastors and very close friends since that connection in October, 1974. Sherlyn and I are forever grateful to God for their friendship and deeply value their input into our lives.

REFLECTION
Why do we need close friends?

We have several other couples with whom we have very close friendships. Friendships like these bring security, protection, and fun into our lives. We have found this to be a vital and necessary part of our lives as leaders.

Leaders work with teams of people every day to fulfill the vision God has given them. This carries a responsibility that only leaders understand. Even though we take days off, we are never really off duty. Therefore, close friendships with other leaders bring a depth of caring and understanding that is necessary for leaders to stay healthy and strong emotionally, physically and mentally.

DAY 3

Be and Remain Teachable

"For I say, through the grace given to me, to everyone who is among you, not think of himself more highly than he ought to think, but to think soberly, as God has dealt to each one a measure of faith" (Romans 12:3 NKJV).

"Do not neglect the gift that is in you, which was given to you by prophecy with the laying on of the hands of the eldership. Meditate on these things; give yourself entirely to them, that your progress may be evident to all. Take heed to yourself and to the doctrine. Continue in them, for in doing this you will save both yourself and those who hear you" (1 Timothy 3: 14-16 NKJV).

> When we think we know more than we do or flaunt a superior attitude and tone, it is difficult for anyone to help us.

Throughout my years of ministry, I have had the privilege to speak into other leaders' lives. Usually they want counsel because either their personal life is falling apart or they are having significant challenges in their church, ministry or business.

On several occasions the leader coming for counsel seems to have all the answers and does most of the talking. It is difficult to help a leader if he or she thinks they have all the answers. I try to listen carefully, and whenever there is the slightest opening in the conversation, I do my best to interject some words that I believe will help. Sometimes I have had to say, "Unless you let me share my thoughts with you, I will not be able to give you any help."

At times I went away from meetings feeling sad, knowing the leaders could not be helped with their issues unless they changed their attitudes and became willing to receive counsel. Many other times I met with leaders who were broken and open to hear what the Holy Spirit was speaking to them. I have seen their lives and ministries change and become fruitful.

When we think we know more than we do or flaunt a superior attitude and tone, it

REFLECTION

When have you benefitted from someone's counsel?

is difficult for anyone to help us. When we say "God told me this or God told me that" it puts up a wall. I want to ask people like that, "Why did you come to me for insight if God already told you." A better way to receive input from someone is to say, "I am having difficulty in this area of my life or ministry, but I don't know why." When we humble ourselves we open the door for wisdom to pour into our lives.

It is important for every leader to have people to whom they can go for wisdom and insight. No leader should think he or she is too important to have this kind of protection.

Build a Strong Team

"As each one has received a gift, minister it to one another, as good stewards of the manifold grace of God. If anyone speaks, let him speak as the oracles of God. If anyone ministers, let him do it as with the ability which God supplies, that in all things God may be glorified through Jesus Christ, to whom belong the glory and the dominion forever and ever. Amen" (1 Peter 4:10-11 NKJV).

> Many times visionary leaders are not detail oriented.

Soon after I took on the responsibility of pastoring a church, I quickly found out that I could not do it myself. Sherlyn and I began to pray for God to send us a strong team of people who had the gifts to help move the vision forward. I needed to surround myself with individuals who were strong in areas in which I was not gifted.

A visionary leader knows where he wants to go, and he wants to get there fast. Visionary leaders, many times, need those on their team who can put together a strategy that shows the how, the when, and the why. Also, many times visionary leaders are not detail oriented.

One time we needed a business administrator for the church. This person needed to oversee all the finances and budgets along with other business-type duties. We prayed that God would send us that person. Several individuals from within the congregation and one from outside the congregation applied for the position. Several applicants said they felt God had told them that they were the one for the position, which made it more difficult for us to make the decision. We met with the individual from outside the congregation and felt he was the one to whom we were to offer the position. We felt a peace in our hearts about our decision. He came and served our congregation faithfully for twenty-one years until his retirement. He did an outstanding job by bringing order, faith and stability to the business and financial areas of the church. One lesson we learned was how important prayer is in these matters.

REFLECTION
What leadership skill is your weakest?

To build a strong team it is important to delegate and empower each person to fulfill his or her assigned responsibilities. I am not a micro-manager by any means.

I have always allowed team members to carve out their areas of ministry. Sometimes that changes. We had a youth pastor who served for nineteen years. He did an outstanding job in giving leadership to the youth ministry in our congregation. He came to me one day and said he sensed a change coming for him. He is a very creatively gifted person. Immediately I felt he would be the person to oversee the largest building project we have ever done. As he worked alongside the architects, the design for our building was created. When people comment on the design and beauty of our building, my response always is that the former youth pastor's finger prints are all over our building.

To build a strong team the leader of the team needs to let each team member functions in his or her strength. Some leaders think they need to be strong in each area. No, we need to stay in our strengths and recognize no one is strong in every area. Leaders need to be secure enough to empower others so that together a vision can be fulfilled. Insecurities in leaders have aborted many visions.

Embrace the Whole Body of Christ

DAY 5

"John said to Jesus, 'Teacher, we saw someone using your name to cast out demons, but we told him to stop because he wasn't in our group.' 'Don't stop him!'Jesus said. 'No one who performs a miracle in my name will

18

soon be able to speak evil of me. Anyone who is not against us is for us. If anyone gives you even a cup of water because you belong to the Messiah, I tell you the truth, that person will surely be rewarded'" (Mark 9:38-40 NLT).

The body of Christ is made up of many different groups and streams of ministry. These groups have different slants on doctrine and use different methods in ministering to people. We get into trouble when we think we are the only group that has everything right. We then get into exclusivity, thinking we have an edge on understanding the Bible. This kind of attitude puts walls up between groups in the body of Christ. God has set in His body different strengths and groups

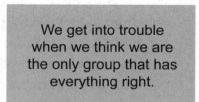

We get into trouble when we think we are the only group that has everything right.

with a particular emphasis to bring a truth or an area of ministry needed by the body.

Several years ago, I was in a meeting when a discussion put a negative implication on several particular ministries. These ministries have strengths and strategies from which the whole body could benefit if we would be humble enough to receive from one another. I spoke up in that meeting saying I feel uncomfortable saying things about good ministries that put them in a negative light. Through the years I have invited ministers from various streams of ministry to speak to our congregation. This has been a positive thing for us.

Some years ago I heard that a minister from a neighboring town was saying negative things about our church. I found out that pastor's church was building a new church building. I felt impressed to send that church an offering for their building. In response, the pastor called me. We had lunch together and became acquainted with each other

REFLECTION
Why is being independent dangerous?

and the churches we pastored. At the end of our lunch, we admitted that even though we have some doctrinal differences, one thing we can agree on is that we both want to reach people with the gospel of Jesus Christ. We made a commitment to each other that rather than speak ill of each other, we would pray for each other. This is the attitude we need to have in the Body of Christ.

It is not good to be a lone ranger and work independently. I am very thankful for the many ministry connections I have from various streams of ministry, which have been a valuable source of strength for me.

For many years a group of ministers in our area, from various denominations, have gathered regularly to pray together for our community and for each other. I am also thankful for the network of ministers from where I receive my ministerial credentials . . . the oversight, accountability, and relational strength that come through that stream of ministry, I value deeply.

Jesus prayed that we would all be one, just as He and the Father are one—"as you are in Me, Father, and I am in you. And may they be one in us so that the world will believe you sent me."

DAY 6

Family First

"He must manage his own family well, having children who respect and obey him. For if a man cannot manage his own household, how can he take care of God's church?" (1Timothy 3:4-5 NLT).

"I have singled him out so that he will direct his sons and their families to keep the way of the Lord by doing what is right and just. Then I will do for Abraham all that I have promised" (Genesis 18:19 NLT).

Since the beginning of taking on the role as lead pastor, Sherlyn and I

> When I got off the phone, I was reminded in my heart, family first.

decided our family comes before our church responsibilities. That meant being there for them, to care for them, and meet the needs they had. When our son was on the basketball team at his school, we made great effort to be at the games. When our daughters had special things in which they were involved, we attended their functions. This does not mean we did everything right or that our children were perfect. In conversations with our children as adults, they shared some of the things they felt growing up. My wife and I had underestimated the pressures they felt by being the pastor's children. Now Sherlyn and I realize that we should have been more sensitive to our children's feelings during those years.

When our children were growing up, I traveled quite a bit to other nations. If I could do it over, I would do less traveling during those crucial years in their lives. On one such trip to Poland, I was scheduled to travel from Sweden to Poland on an eight-hour overnight ferry. In those days communication from Poland to the U.S. was limited, so I called home before I boarded the ferry. When I spoke with Sherlyn, I could tell something was wrong. She did not want to tell me so it wouldn't ruin my trip. I insisted and found out one of my teenage children was having a very difficult time emotionally. When I got off the phone, I was reminded in my heart, family first. I sensed the Holy Spirit saying that I should turn around and go home. The men who were traveling with me reminded me that we had a ten-day itinerary to fulfill. I told them about my commitment to my family. My traveling companions said if I felt I should go home then I should go. I did.

When I got home, I realized I made the right decision. Sherlyn and I took our teenager away for a few days to determine what needed to be done to bring healing and hope to her. Our child went through a number of years trying to deal with the emotional side of life but is healthy and doing well today.

The lesson I learned from that experience is when we make a commitment to put family first, it will be tested. We have always stood by our children through the choices they have made in their lives. The pressure they felt growing up as pastor's kids was very real to them, and we did not see it as well as we should have. Today our children are all doing well, and we have solid relationships with them.

Sherlyn and I counsel pastor couples to pay close attention to their children.

REFLECTION
Do your children know they are more important than the ministry you lead?

Spend time with them away from ministry responsibilities. Listen to what they are saying and feeling. Do not disconnect from them.

Live and Minister Caleb's Way

DAY 7

In Numbers 14:24 (NKJV) we read, "But My servant Caleb, because he has a different spirit in him and has followed me fully, I will bring into the land where he went, and his descendants shall inherit it."

God had promised the land of Canaan to the children of Israel. Moses sent out twelve spies to check out the land to see what the land was like. Did it have walled cities? What kind of people were there? After forty days the twelve spies came back and gave a report of what they saw. Ten of the spies brought back a bad report saying there is no way we can take the land, because it has walled cities and giants live in the land. Caleb quieted the people and said, "Let us go up at once, and take possession, for we are well able to overcome it." Ten said there is no way we can do this and two said we can do this. Two different opinions were being voiced to Moses and the people.

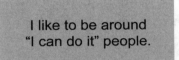

I like to be around "I can do it" people.

The ten who said we cannot do this swayed the people and the children of Israel spent forty years in the wilderness. A thirteen-day journey became forty years of wandering in the wilderness. The families of the ten who said we cannot do it died in the wilderness.

Forty-five years later Caleb approached Joshua, who was now leading the children of Israel, and asked for the land Moses had promised him. Caleb said, "And now, behold, the Lord has kept me alive, as He said, these forty-five years, ever since the Lord spoke this word to Moses while Israel wandered in the wilderness; and now, here I am this day, eighty-five years old. As yet I am as strong this day as on the day that Moses sent me."

When I get to heaven, I want to have a cup of tea with Caleb and ask him how he put up with all those murmuring people for forty-five years. What made the difference in

Caleb? He saw things different from the crowd. His positive attitude and approach toward life kept him above the circumstances of life. He did not have a victim mentality like the other spies did. I like to be around "I can do it" people.

This is the kind of attitude leaders must have to fulfill their assignments from God. When leaders display this kind of attitude and approach to ministry, they inspire and give hope to people. When Sherlyn and I went to Bible School, we began to understand who we are in Christ. This understanding built within us an attitude and spiritual strength that has sustained us through many challenging times. To maintain this kind of approach to life we must continually feed our spirit the Word of God.

REFLECTION
How do we turn negative attitudes into positive ones?

When we built our last church facility, we were led to build it during an economic downturn. Some thought we were making a mistake. But as we moved ahead sensing God's direction, we realized there were many blessings attached to doing the project at that time: Building prices were good, and we were able to supply jobs for people who otherwise would not have had jobs during that time.

CHAPTER 2

Overcoming Discouragement and Other Things I Learned

Sam Smucker

Swim in Your Own Lane

DAY 1

"Oh, don't worry; we wouldn't dare say that we are as wonderful as these other men who tell you how important they are! But they are only comparing themselves with each other, using themselves as the standard of measurement. How ignorant!" (2 Corinthians 10:12 NLT).

In our second year of pastoring, we took forty people on our first mission trip to Jamaica. I had been introduced to a man by the name of V.T. Williams who had a vibrant crusade and church-planting ministry. He invited us to bring a team from our church to erect a church building in the Kingston area and help with a crusade on the other side of the island. About half the team accompanied my wife and me to the crusade. About 5,000 people attended each evening during the weeklong crusade. I had never preached to a crowd that large. In my heart I was hoping that V.T. would ask me to preach one of the nights, but, at the same time, I was scared to do it. Sure enough one morning he asked me if I wanted to preach that evening. I said I would. I was extremely nervous about it. All of my ministry life I have always had to overcome the fear of speaking in front of people.

> In twenty minutes I ran out of things to say.

That night I preached. Being very young in ministry, I thought I should minister like V.T. does. So I began to preach like he did (V.T. is an old time revivalist). In twenty minutes I ran out of things to say. I didn't know what to do so I thought I would have an altar call for people to make a commitment to Jesus Christ. About twenty people came forward. I prayed with them. Then V.T. got up and preached about ten minutes. He gave an altar call and hundreds of people came forward. I was discouraged and felt as if I didn't do a good job in ministering to that group of people.

The next morning when we were eating breakfast with V.T., he said something to me that I will never forget. He said, "Pastor Sam, swim in your own lane." I did not know what he meant. Then he said, "Be yourself, we all have different gifts that God gives us. In swimming competitions it is very important for each swimmer to stay within his or her lane."

Previously I had struggled by comparing myself with other pastors and with other churches, but that day, I was set free in my heart from trying to copy someone else. Psalm 139:16 NLT says, "You saw me before I was born. Every day of my life was recorded in your book. Every moment was laid out before a single day had passed."

REFLECTION
Do you know the swim lane "assigned" to you?

We all have an assignment from God to fulfill. You might say, "I don't know what that is." That's all right; help someone else fulfill their assignment. Invest yourself in someone else's vision and that will become a seedbed for your calling. Be real, be authentic. Don't try to be someone else. Proverbs 18:16 says, "A man's gift makes room for itself." Your gift will shine and make room for itself. That lesson has helped me stay within my calling during my ministry years.

Loyalty

Being loyal is defined in the dictionary as "faithful to a cause, ideal, or custom." It can mean being faithful to a private person to whom fidelity is held to be due.

Loyalty can be seen, for example, in longevity where someone has worked with you faithfully for many years.

I have been blessed to have several individuals work with me for more than thirty years. Through those years a trust developed among us that has brought great strength and stability to Worship Center, where I have served as lead pastor for thirty-eight years. These individuals and their wives have worked alongside us through the good times and the difficult times. We have developed a trust that goes deep into our hearts. Leaders need other leaders around them who understand their personality and their style. When criticism raises its ugly head, those who are loyal to one another will stand together. When there are differences of opinion in making a decision, they are not afraid to have some conflict in meetings where strong heartfelt discussions are necessary. Then when decisions are made, the team stands together on the decisions.

The Apostle Paul had individuals who turned on him when he took a stand for the gospel of Jesus Christ. Paul talks about a man named Demas who deserted him. He talks about Alexander the coppersmith who did him much harm. He talks about others who abandoned him.

Paul says in Colossians 4:7-9 (NLT), "Tychicus will give you a full report about how I am getting along. He is a beloved brother and faithful helper who serves with me in the Lord's work. I have sent him to you for this very purpose—to let you know how we are doing and to encourage you. I am also sending Onesimus, a faithful and beloved brother, one of our own people." Beloved and faithful are stated in these verses several times. So then loyalty is developed when individuals have a deep love for one another and that produces a faithfulness toward each other that has a very strong bond.

A person I trusted was not loyal to our church values.

Some years ago we asked someone to come on our team to take responsibility for a certain area of the ministry. Things went well for quite a long time until this person did some things in that area of ministry that violated our ministry's values. When we approached this person about it, he promised us that it would not happen again. But several months later the same things happened. We no longer had confidence in that person to lead that area of ministry, so we asked for his resignation. Instead of admitting to the inappropriate actions, the individual chose to get as many people on his side as possible. It was a difficult time for the church to go through. Although that individual and family moved out of the area, they returned several years later and apologized for their actions. We were able to bring closure to the situation.

That is an example of a time when a person I trusted was not loyal to our church values. I learned through that situation that disloyalty in someone's heart can be destructive to a church and to the individual.

REFLECTION
How does disloyalty cause destruction to the church?

Loyalty is developed in relationships and with a team of people working together when we have love for each other that goes deeper than the differences of opinion. Out of that love develops a faithfulness that is very strong and not easily broken with one another.

Overcome Discouragement

DAY 3

"So Moses told the children of Israel what the Lord had said, but they refused to listen anymore. They had become too discouraged by brutality of their slavery"(Exodus 6:9 NLT).

Jesus said to him, "If you can believe, all things are possible to him who believes." Immediately the father of the child cried out and said with tears, "Lord I believe; help my unbelief!" (Mark 9:23-24 NKJV).

Discouragement comes knocking on all our doors. While serving as a pastor for 38 years, I have had times when discouragement tried to put me down. The pressures of working with the needs of people can deposit a layer of residue on our hearts that weighs on us. Sometimes the persons who come to you for help start blaming you for their problems because you didn't say what they wanted to hear. When discouragement begins to set in, problems are magnified in our minds and things begin to look worse than they really are. We are like the man that came to Jesus with a demon-possessed son and said, "I believe, help my unbelief." We want to believe but somehow the hope and the strength to believe is depleted.

> The pressures of working with the needs of people can deposit a layer of residue on our hearts that weighs on us..

Some years ago I allowed discouragement to set in. We were dealing with some intense family issues; in addition, my father had died at age sixty-nine, and the work of pastoring a growing church seemed too demanding. I wanted to throw in the towel and quit. My feelings really scared me. I had never felt that way before. I met with the elders of the church and shared my heart with them. I told them I needed some time off for my emotional and mental health and asked if they would give me a three-month paid sabbatical. They graciously allowed our family to take three months off. I scheduled ministers, some from our staff and some from the outside, for the preaching while I was gone. Our family did extensive travelling around the country, attended several conferences, had an extended family vacation, and I participated in a personal prayer retreat. It was a much needed time of refreshing for us, and we came back encouraged.

After Sherlyn and I came back from the three months off, we realized this was something all our full-time pastors needed. We established a sabbatical policy, which grants all full-time pastors a seven-week sabbatical every seven years. The sabbatical is for rest, extended family time, and refueling emotionally and spiritually. This benefit to our pastors has been a good thing. We also provide a certain amount of funds for travel expenses. I encourage this for all pastors.

When we get discouraged, we stop believing that good things will happen for us. When we lose hope, the enemy comes in and gets us so discouraged we stop believing. When we stop believing, we don't give God anything to work with in our hearts. We need

REFLECTION
Do you struggle with discouragement?

to be encouraged in the inner man so we can believe again. Jesus said, "All things are possible to him who believeth."

Several things to do when we become discouraged: 1) Get with friends and be honest with them. 2) Go away somewhere to clear your mind and emotions. 3) Read the

Word of God and let the Holy Spirit stir up your faith again. 4) Pray and ask God to renew your vision.

Speak Faith

One day Jesus and His disciples were walking toward Jerusalem. Jesus was hungry. He saw a fig tree at a distance, but when He got to the tree there were no figs. Jesus said to the tree, "No one will eat fruit from you ever again." Jesus' disciples heard him speak to the tree. The next morning, as they passed by the fig tree, they noticed it had dried up from the roots. Peter, who remembered what Jesus had said to the tree, said, "Rabbi, look! The fig tree which You cursed has withered away."

Jesus answered, "Have faith in God. For assuredly, I say to you, whoever says to this mountain, be removed and be cast into the sea, and does not doubt in his heart, but believes that those things he says will be done, he will have whatever he says" (Mark 11:22-23 NKJV).

> The leader's words can be full of faith or full of fear, they can encourage or discourage.

Jesus was demonstrating to His disciples how powerful words can be when we speak something we believe in our hearts. Sometimes we have doubt in our mind, but in our heart we know what God is saying. Words of faith go deep into the core of the issues of life. The fig tree withered from the roots up.

The words of a leader influence a big part of his or her leadership. The leader's words can be full of faith or full of fear, they can encourage or discourage. When a leader speaks confidently about what he or she believes—those words carry creative power.

About fifteen years ago, we began to plan for a new facility for our congregation. We were making good progress toward our vision until we encountered some zoning issues that took four and a half years to resolve. Our faith was tested as a team, but we kept believing and saying we will build this building.

After the zoning issues were resolved, we took a fresh look at the building plans and decided to change the plans, which required another two years for approval. When we were ready to break ground, the economy took a nose dive. Although it did not look like a good time to build, we felt led by the Holy Spirit to move ahead and were able to supply jobs for workers who otherwise would have been laid off of their jobs. We were able to negotiate good prices for the building materials. Seventeen months later we moved into our new facility. At this point, we have been in the building almost five years and have sixty-five percent

REFLECTION
How are your words affecting others?

of it paid. I say, "With the eye of faith we see that building totally paid."

When the Holy Spirit gives a vision, it is important to believe it, speak faith and take a step of faith. When your faith is tested, keep believing and speaking the same thing. Your heart and your mouth need to be in agreement. Speaking your faith is to speak the end desired result even when you don't see it with your physical eyes. Before we started the building whenever I drove by the property, I would say to the people in the car, "Do you see that building in that field?" They would ask, "What building?" I answered, "With the eye of faith I see a building that will be a ministry base for our congregation." I spoke that many times before I actually saw it with my physical eyes.

God told Abraham, whatever you can see, that is what I will give you. As leaders, let us not be afraid to speak faith.

Take Care of Yourself

"Guard your heart above all else, for it determines the course of your life" (Proverbs 4:23 NLT).

The Apostles returned to Jesus from their ministry tour and told him all they had done and taught. Then Jesus said, "Let's go off by ourselves to a quiet place and rest awhile." He said this because there were so many people coming and going that Jesus and His disciples didn't even have time to eat" (Mark 6:30-31 NLT).

Serving as a leader carries many responsibilities with it. Balancing marriage, family, and ministry along with staying sharp in our personal relationship with the Lord in devotion and study is something we must manage with wisdom. If we are not paying attention to having balance in our lives, stress can take a toll and result in burnout.

About fifteen years ago something happened to me that got my attention. I had been doing a lot of traveling to other nations. I had made eighteen trips to India, a nation I love to travel to, so this trip was not something new to me. On my way to the Philadelphia airport, I began to feel very anxious. I didn't understand the reason for my anxiety but thought maybe I needed something to eat. My brother and his wife were traveling with me, and we stopped to get something to eat. That did not help ease my anxiety, but we continued to the airport. I dropped the passengers off at the terminal and went to park my car in the long-term parking area. On the way back to the terminal, I had to lie down in the shuttle bus because I thought I was going to pass out. I got to the terminal, checked in, and went toward the gate. As I got closer to the gate I again felt as if I was about to pass out, so I lay down on the floor. When people saw me, they came running and asked if I was OK. I said, "No, I am not."

> When people saw me, they came running and asked if I was OK.

They called 911, and I was loaded in an ambulance. I told my brother and his wife to proceed with the trip. Later, they told me that my speech was slurred, which is a symptom of a stroke. The ambulance transported me to the hospital where I had tests. Doctors could not find anything amiss but kept me overnight.

The next morning a doctor came to my room. He asked what I was afraid of and if this was my first trip to India. He said there is nothing wrong with you physically, but diagnosed my symptoms as a panic and anxiety attack. I was totally taken by surprise.

I found out that my fast-paced lifestyle and the responsibility of the load I was carrying had caught up to me. I hit a wall that I did not know was there. I must admit I did travel to India the next day because I was scheduled to speak at a crusade and at a pastors' conference. Needless to say I am not sure if that was a good decision or not, but the trip went fine.

After that incident, Sherlyn and I decided we need to put some guardrails around my schedule and responsibilities. We became more protective of my days off. We scheduled getaways for her and me on a regular basis. We restructured some things in the

REFLECTION
How do you handle anxiety?

church so I did not have as many staff members reporting to me. Once or twice a year, I also began to take times away by myself for prayer and reflection. That experience taught me a very important lesson: Stress can sneak up on us without us knowing it. We must be proactive in guarding our hearts.

Treasure What Matters Most

DAY 6

"When He saw the crowds, He had compassion on them because they were confused and helpless, like sheep without a shepherd" (Matthew 9:36 NLT).

One day as Jesus was walking along the shore of the Sea of Galilee, he saw two brothers — Simon, also called Peter, and Andrew — throw a net into the water, for they fished for a living. Jesus called out to them, "Come, follow me, and I will show you how to fish for people!" And they left their nets at once and followed him (Matthew 4:18-20 NLT).

> I have had to remind myself sometimes throughout the years that pastoring is all about people.

Never has anyone treasured people like Jesus. He taught His disciples as they traveled with Him. He demonstrated this by stopping to minister to one person and by preaching and teaching to a crowd. Jesus drilled into them day after day that it is all about people—loving, healing, restoring, serving and empowering people. Even on the day He was hanging on the cross, Jesus was praying for the soldiers who had just finished nailing Him to the cross. Jesus spoke to the thieves who were crucified with Him. He saw His mother in the crowd and asked someone to take care of her. Jesus treasured what matters most and stayed focused on that. He understood eternal realities—only people—not things—make it to heaven.

Jesus said in Matthew 6:19-21 NKJV, "Do not lay up for yourselves treasures on earth, where moth and rust destroy and where thieves break in and steal; but lay up for yourselves treasures in heaven, where neither moth nor rust destroys and where thieves do not break in and steal. For where your treasure is, there your heart is also."

We use this portion of scripture many times in sharing about giving and receiving offerings. I believe the treasure talked about in this scripture is referring to investing our lives into people. The only thing we can take with us to heaven is people. People are the most important treasure we have.

I have had to remind myself sometimes throughout the years that pastoring is all about people. I can get caught up in the mechanics of pastoring a church and forget it is all about giving hope, help and healing to people. Even though we have hospital visitation pastors and teams, Sherlyn and I also go and visit people who are hurting because we want to stay in touch with the hurting side of people. Leaders must maintain soft hearts toward hurting people. Jesus was able to love the person

REFLECTION
Do your actions show that you treasure people?

unconditionally even though his or her lifestyle was not good. Jesus looked past the mess a person was in and saw what they could become.

Recently we were with a family who experienced a tragedy. As we were leaving their home, Sherlyn and I both were thanking God for the privilege of speaking life into a family that was hurting very deeply. When we as leaders rub shoulders with those who experience the deepest heartache and disappointments, we ourselves stay softhearted and always ready to be carriers of hope and healing. When we isolate ourselves from the hurting and think we are too important to spend time with those who are broken, we harden our hearts toward those who need us the most.

Succession and Change

"Now Joshua son of Nun was full of the spirit of wisdom, for Moses had laid his hands on him. So the people of Israel obeyed him, doing just as the Lord had commanded Moses" (Deuteronomy 34:9 NLT).

"I tell you the truth, anyone who believes in Me will do the same works I have done, and even greater works, because I am going to the Father" (John 14:12 NLT).

Succession and change are inevitable because we all get older and will leave this earth. Leaders build ministries and organizations that make an impact on people's lives and on society. Therefore, as a pastor I realized that it is important for me to prepare the church for change and succession.

When I took the responsibility to serve as lead pastor, I somehow sensed that I would serve in that capacity for forty years. Of course, at that time, forty years was so far off that it seemed like an eternity. A few years ago when we hit the thirty-five year mark, I started to realize succession will be a reality.

In the by-laws of our church, we have written guidelines for succession. We began a four-and-a-half year succession plan. As I am writing this chapter, we are two years into that plan. We have selected my successor. During the next two-and-a-half years, I will mentor and walk alongside this individual. In our case, the successor is someone who has been part of our congregation since he was a child. We are looking forward to having a good, positive transition.

> People have come up to me and said, "You can never retire."

Succession planning is very important for the ongoing success of a church. Many people do not like change. Therefore, a prayerfully thought-out plan is necessary so the congregation can embrace the changes. Many transitions in churches are too abrupt, which make it hard for the congregation to adjust and result in some people leaving rather than dealing with the pain of change. I encourage every church to intentionally plan for succession and not wait for a forced succession.

People have come up to me and said, "You can never retire." I noticed most of the people who say that are retired. I personally don't look at retirement as doing nothing. Sherlyn and I will transition into spending our time pouring our lives into other leaders. We will stay in the church and be an ongoing part of this church family. We look forward to how the Lord will continue to build the church through the new lead pastor and his team. It is important that the new lead pastor embraces the vision of the church and knows the DNA of the church. Methods and style will change, but the vision of the church needs to remain strong. It is also important that the outgoing lead pastor is honored appropriately so the congregation knows he or she is treated in a good way.

About fifteen years ago, I began to see that the leadership of our church was getting older. We were not engaging enough of the emerging generations in leadership positions. We intentionally began to pray about this and ask younger individuals to be a part of our staff, board of directors, various committees and teams. Our church today has a good mixture of younger and older staff members. This has brought a new vitality and perspective into the leadership and vision of the church.

REFLECTION
How do you view retirement?

For a church to continue to grow and be successful in fulfilling its assignment from God, change is inevitable and can launch the church into future success.

CHAPTER 3

Life-long Learning
and
Team Dynamics

Barry Wissler

Become a Life-long Learner

Scripture teaches that we are all called to be disciples and to make disciples, but what is a disciple? Someone who accepts a free offer to go to heaven? Or, someone who attends meetings every week? The word disciple comes from the Latin word for *learner*. If we stop learning, we stop growing. We begin to coast instead of excel. I believe the more we learn, the more effective we can be. This is true in any area of our lives.

The desire to do things ourselves starts when we are two years old. But, no matter what our age, we can learn a lot from others. Imagine trying to learn to cook without a teacher or a recipe book? You would have to experiment with all the raw ingredients to see what works. But if your mom teaches you, you take a class or at least read a cookbook, you are more apt to become a good cook much faster.

No one lives long enough to learn everything they need to learn starting from scratch. To be successful, we learn from others. We search for people who have already paid the price to learn the things that we need to know in order to achieve our goals.

I want to challenge you to become a life-long learner and to continue to develop yourself. Just like those running a race, those in leadership are tempted to fall into a pattern of coasting and not pressing toward the goal.

Many Christians have a bias against education, assuming that everything we need will somehow just fall out of heaven. Acts 7:22 (ESV) says, "Moses was educated in all the learning of the Egyptians, and he was a man of power in words and deeds. Why does the Bible mention this? Why did God send Moses to school in Egypt? What could he have possibly learned in the Egyptian school that could help him lead Israel?

> Many Christians have a bias against education. . . .

We must see all truth as God's truth. The world is full of things to learn and discover. One of the saddest things is when people settle for what they currently know. Although some never have a chance to learn, many Christians have the opportunity but choose not to. Some Christians have full hearts but empty heads. We do not want a Christianity that is only cerebral; however, passionate love for God should not be void of knowledge. Proverbs says repeatedly that fools hate knowledge; it also says that wise men store up knowledge.

In the Bible, we notice that the greatest leaders never stopped developing. Moses picked up a whole new set of skills at age forty, and assumed his major leadership role at age 80. Abraham became a world traveler at age 70, and became a father two decades later. Paul went to the desert to get his head on straight after his Damascus road experience, an event that caused him to rethink his theology and his life mission. He reordered his life goals and beliefs in the middle of his life. He didn't even begin his missionary journeys until his mid-forties.

REFLECTION
How are you becoming a life-long learner?

Remember, there are many ways to learn. Many learn better from people rather than books. A coach or mentor can often teach us a lot. Professional sports teams have several coaches, who each specialize in one thing. The athletes are professionals yet still need coaches to help them. Why do ministry leaders think that we do not need coaches? The goal for every leader is to find out what they need to learn and then find out where they can learn it.

We All Are Better on a Team

DAY 2

Important work is best accomplished by teams. Sometimes leaders feel that to be successful, they need to learn how to do everything well. They try to improve their weak areas. While this is good, there are some things we will simply never be great at doing, which is why we need others. God has designed us to need others and gave each of us strengths that others need. We are instructed in scripture to never say, "I have no need of you."

We use teamwork in athletics and even in business, but for some reason, ministry is often seen as an individual task that focuses on the calling and work of one person. I think we would be more effective if we approached ministry with a team mentality. Teams allow for specialization, collaboration and take advantage of a variety of gifting.

Have you ever thought about the fact that God himself is a team? Yes, He is one God but in three persons. I believe that He models teamwork for us in the way the Trinity has specialization of labor. We even see Father God as a team leader with Jesus and the Holy Spirit in submission to Him. Yet all three are equally God and all are involved in the purposes of God. In the beginning God said, "Let us make man." We see that the Creator Father, the Holy Spirit and Jesus the Eternal Word, were all present at creation. At the baptism of Jesus, we also notice that they all were present. In the story and plan of redemption, we see three persons working together in complementary ways.

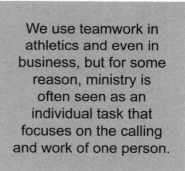

We use teamwork in athletics and even in business, but for some reason, ministry is often seen as an individual task that focuses on the calling and work of one person.

We see the early church working together in teams. They formed a team to feed the widows who were being neglected. Peter and John healed the sick together. Paul and Barnabas handled finances together for accountability in Acts 11. Decisions about the ordination and sending of missionaries were made by a team in Acts 13. And in 2 Corinthians 2:12, Paul was unwilling to accept an invitation to do ministry without Titus being able to help him. The early church did not have an individualistic approach to ministry. There was a variety of gifts and ministries, and always a plurality of the leadership offices. In fact, nearly every time offices and gifts are mentioned, it is plural rather than singular.

Consider this wisdom from Ecclesiastes 4:9-12, "Two are better than one because they have a good return for their labor. For if either of them falls, the one will lift up his companion. But woe to the one who falls when there is not another to lift him up. Furthermore, if two lie down together they keep warm, but how can one be warm alone? And if one can overpower him who is alone, two can resist him. A cord of three strands is not quickly torn apart."

REFLECTION

Do you believe you need to do everything well by yourself or do you use the strengths of others?

In the last days, we will become more aware that we need each other. We all need companionship. We will all have times when we need someone to pick us up. Spiritual warfare is not an individual sport. We fight together and we stand together. We will also win together and complete the Great Commission together.

Build a Functional Team

DAY 3

When selecting team members, character is more important than gifting and skills. More important than having gifting and skills is that team members must have the right character, the right heart and godly motives.

Alan Vincent, my spiritual father, always used David's formation of a team of mighty men as an example. David had more than thirty men who he called his mighty men. They were all capable leaders, who could have been leading elsewhere but chose to follow David because they believed in David and his vision.

We read in 1 Chronicles 12:17 (NASB), "David went out to meet them, and said to them, 'If you come peacefully to me to help me, my heart shall be united with you; but if to betray me to my adversaries, since there is no wrong in my hands, may the God of our fathers look on it and decide.'"

From this we can form three questions that are useful in assessing the character and motivations of team members: First, "Have you come peacefully?" In the English language, peace usu-

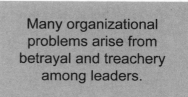

Many organizational problems arise from betrayal and treachery among leaders.

ally means absence of conflict but in ancient languages, the word peace was used in the context of relationships. The Greek word for peace, *Irene*, was used to speak of a mended relationship that had been formerly hostile. It was used as a medical term for a bone that was broken; after it healed, it was said to have "come to peace." Just like a reconciled relationship, a bone is stronger after the break is healed.

In essence David was saying, "Will you come with the attitude to strengthen relationships between us? Because if you come to cause turbulence in our relationships, we don't need you even if you are gifted."

The second question is "Have you come to help me?" Are you here to become part of our team in order to get our job done or are you only here for your own reasons.? Do you have your own agenda or are you willing to join with the agenda of the team?

REFLECTION
Do you exhibit honesty, openness and loyalty?

Paul could delegate many things to Timothy because he had the right kind of heart: "For I have no one else of kindred spirit who will genuinely be concerned for your welfare. For they all seek after their own interests, not those of Christ Jesus."

A good creed for leadership teams is found in Philippians 2:1-7 (NASB), "Make my joy complete by being of the same mind, maintaining the same love, united in spirit, intent on one purpose. Do nothing from selfishness or empty conceit, but with humility of mind regard one another as more important than yourselves; do not merely look out for your own personal interests, but also for the interests of others. Have this attitude in yourselves which was also in Christ Jesus, who, although He existed in the form of God, did not regard equality with God a thing to be grasped, but emptied Himself, taking the form of a bond-servant."

The third question is "Will you let your heart be joined to mine?" David wanted a relationship with his leaders and for great teams to become friends. Trust enables honesty, openness, and loyalty. In order for a team to be joined at the heart level, there must be a commitment to invest time and a willingness to be vulnerable.

David ends by giving a clear warning: "if you betray me to my enemies, since there is no wrong (violence) in my hands, may God look and bring judgment." David is basically saying that if a person is saying yes to those three things, he is going to trust that person and give them a place on the team; but if they break that trust and betray him, God will see this. Many organizational problems arise from betrayal and treachery among leaders.

Team Meeting Protocol

DAY 4

One challenge for every team is to make good decisions and maintain unity over decisions. If team members are not honest and do not engage in debate, then real teamwork will probably not be possible. Some leaders surround themselves with servants who rarely disagree or ask difficult questions. That may be easier for the leader, but rarely yields quality decisions and can undermine unity over time.

Team members need to know that they are heard and that it is okay to ask questions. Hard questions can lead to better decisions because time is spent looking at possible outcomes and planning ahead to prevent problems in executing a decision.

It is possible to have unfiltered discussions where team members wrestle with various options and opinions and still arrive at a decision with which everyone can agree. Once a decision is made, the team can speak with one voice and execute the decision together. This requires that team members trust each other enough to be honest. Without trust and honesty, the process is hindered.

> Some leaders surround themselves with servants who rarely disagree or ask difficult questions.

Individual opinions rarely express the full council of God; therefore, everyone needs to listen to each other. Nobody is the final spokesperson for God, even if they are convinced they are right. No opinion, caution, or position should be discounted; all should be brought to the table freely. Disagreements can be very productive as they can help the team arrive at the best decision. Everyone needs to be heard. After team members have expressed themselves, they should allow others to do the same. No one should dominate the discussion. This requires discipline for those who talk a lot to actually remain silent long enough for others to also express their thoughts.

A person's membership on any team should never be leveraged as a way of advancing personal interest. A person's role on a team is to hear God and decide what is best for the team and the whole organization.

"Do nothing from selfish ambition or conceit, but in humility count others more significant than yourselves. Let each of you look not only to his own interests, but also to the interests of others" (Philippians 2:3, 4 ESV).

This means that we should not be using our position to make things better for ourselves, our department or our cause. Group deliberation enables a team to come into alignment with what God will supply as His one purpose and united position. We only "win" together. Any person who tries to "win" alone can cause the whole team to lose. Disagreements will happen. When they do, it is important for the team not to walk away from the table. They must listen, pray, and deliberate until a decision is reached that reflects God's will and the heart of the team.

A good team has honest discussion, disagreements and deliberations. It is critical that team comments stay with the team. Team members who complain to non-team members about the process or the decisions will erode trust and hinder future discussion and decisions.

REFLECTION
How do you handle disagreements among team members?

Confidentiality about the discussion should be maintained. All opinions on any decision should be shared as part of the process, or not shared at all. Dissenting opinions that are not shared during the process, but are later shared with others outside the meeting, will cause polarization within the larger organization and eventually division within the leadership team.

Success Requires a Successor

DAY 5

"So this joy of mine is now complete. He must increase, but I must decrease" (John 3: 29-30 NASB).

The most obvious test of success as a leader concerns how the organization fares, and what happens under our watch. But the final test of leadership is what happens when we leave our post. A wise leader will not create an unhealthy dependence on himself to the point that the organization cannot do well without him. Very commonly, leaders fail to adequately prepare for their departure.

> Many times out of insecurity, people protect their positions and work so that they feel needed.

It is important for leaders at every level of an organization to constantly train others to do what they do. However, many times out of insecurity, people protect their position and work so that they feel needed. For growth, it is necessary to have a vision for multiplication of leaders at every level. We should work our way out of our jobs. Often if we do this, God will give us another assignment.

The most important transition of course is the selection and training of a successor. For the health of the organization it is not as simple as an announcement of retirement or change of roles. The transition of the primary leader requires time, planning, and the agreement and preparation of many others.

I had founded and pastored a church for 37 years, but recently passed on the role of senior pastor to the executive pastor. The change of roles was expected and planned for a period of eight years. While this amount of time may be considered a luxury and unnecessary, it enabled me as the founding pastor to select a successor and slowly release responsibility to him. Several years before the actual event, a plan was put on paper and agreed upon by the elders, outside overseers, and eventually the whole congregation. The release of authority was also done in stages so that by the time of the installation service, the transfer was a mere formality. Everything but the title had already been carefully passed to the incoming pastor.

REFLECTION
Are you afraid to relinquish responsibility when you know that you should?

We use the word transition to simply communicate the actual change of leaders itself. A transition should be a transition. By definition, a transition is a process. What is practiced most in a relay race is transition, because it is so important to success. When a relay runner passes off the baton, there is a point in time when the transaction occurs. But there is also a period where both runners are running together and the passing is done while both are moving together.

It's best for the runner passing the baton to do so while still running full speed ahead. Unfortunately many leaders often wait until they are too tired to keep running to pass off the baton. The amount of time needed for successful transition may vary according to the organization or the situation. But many transitions would go much smoother if extra time was taken for incremental steps toward the final event.

There are challenges for both the leader who is leaving his post and the leader stepping into his shoes. But time, thought, and planning allow for changes to take place among the leaders involved before the transfer takes place publicly. Allowing time for the transition also allows for internal changes within the organization, as other leaders and volunteers adjust their loyalties and commitments to the new leader. The emotional bond that followers have with their leader must shift to a new person. Part of the plan for the leader, who is exiting his position, is to carefully yet intentionally shift the emotional bond in the hearts of the volunteers to the new leader. That requires that the outgoing leader is secure and willing to make the necessary adjustments internally and organizationally. Don't wait too long. Begin selecting, training and transitioning early.

Don't Leave Without Him

In Exodus 33 God told Moses to lead his people onward and promised to send an angel with them. While most of us would be thrilled with this kind of promise, Moses would not go until God promised that His own presence would accompany him.

"Then Moses said to the Lord, 'See, You say to me, "Bring up this people!" But You Yourself have not let me know whom You will send with me. Moreover, You have said, "I have known you by name, and you have also found favor in My sight."' . . . "And He said, 'My presence shall go with you, and I will give you rest.' Then he said to Him, 'If Your presence does not go with us, do not lead us up from here.'

"'For how then can it be known that I have found favor in Your sight, I and Your people? Is it not by Your going with us, so that we, I and Your people, may be distinguished from all the other people who are upon the face of the earth?' The Lord said to Moses, 'I will also do this thing of which you have spoken; for you have found favor in My sight and I have known you by name'" (Exodus 33:12-17 NASB).

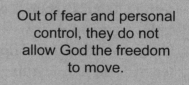

Out of fear and personal control, they do not allow God the freedom to move.

This discussion shows Moses prevailing upon God for grace (favor and ability) that comes from God's presence. Moses did not want to lead without God's presence. That is true humility. Moses was educated in Egypt and raised in the best opportunities available. He had already proven his leadership ability in leading Israel to this point, out of

Egypt. But he knew that he needed the presence of God to fulfill his calling.

I have seen leaders have the opportunity for the presence of God to manifest in their organization and ministry. And yet out of fear and personal control, they do not allow God the freedom to move. They simply will not set aside their own plans and programs enough to allow God's presence to sweep through and fill their work.

It's amazing what men and women can do without God when they just utilize the abilities and skills God has given them. But is this all we want? Will this accomplish the true work of God? Moses insisted it is the presence of God that distinguishes us from others.

It is possible to have a great organization or even a seemingly great church service without God. With the technology and ability, we can do a lot today without God. Or can we? Actually scripture says that our work will be tested by fire and anything of eternal value is going to have its foundation in God and His work and presence.

In Zachariah 4:6 God said, "Not by might nor by power, but by my Spirit," says the Lord Almighty.

REFLECTION

When have you accomplished something using your ability rather than drawing on God's strength?

In this declaration the Hebrew word translated might is *hayil*, which was used to describe military strength, human abilities and wealth. While God gives us resources and uses our abilities, He rejects them as the foundation that will accomplish His work. The word translated power is *koah* and is used to speak of the strength of the load bearers or human determination. We can accomplish a lot by determination, but God also rejects this. Neither our resources nor our determination can finish the house of God.

God wants to give us grace and ability through His presence. Yet many sing about amazing grace applying it only to salvation. Too often it is assumed that we walk out our calling in our own strength, but God offers us so much more!

Failure of Nerve

Imagine being on a football team and experiencing a bone-crushing tackle. Imagine that this tackle does not come from the other team but from one of your own teammates! Imagine being in a war and seeing some of your own fellow soldiers being shot by other soldiers from your own army! It is tragic, but things like this happen in organizations more than we care to admit.

There are two sides to spiritual abuse, the first being when leaders abuse their people. The other side is something that we do not hear much about: it is when someone within an organization becomes destructive to the leader or to the organization. Church leaders call them "clergy killers." They are the people who prey on church leaders (probably unknowingly) and wear them out. Some people are divisive, some are deceptive, some outright destructive. Some spread ideas or teachings that have a destructive effect on the organization.

A book on leadership, *Failure of Nerve* by Edwin H. Friedman talks about the need for what the author calls "nerve to oppose destructive forces at work among people." Friedman calls it "organizational terrorism." For this kind of terrorism to be effective, three emotional prerequisites always persist in a relational system.

Church leaders call them "clergy killers."

First, there must be a sense that no one is in charge. In other words, the overall emotional atmosphere must convey that there is no leader with enough nerve to say *no*.

Second, the system must be vulnerable to a hostage situation. That is, its leaders must be hamstrung by a vulnerability of their own. When leaders are expected always be tolerant and gentle, they are never free to confront wrongdoing.

Third, there must be, among both the leaders and those they lead, an unreasonable faith in "being reasonable." This prevents leaders from taking a stand, which will be construed as being unreasonable with somebody.

Years ago, while I was taking Hebrew at Westminster Seminary, I was shocked when my professor, who was an NIV translator, told me that the name Jezebel means "Where's the Prince?" Those who are master manipulators will aim their venom at the leader who has the nerve to take a stand.

"Be on guard for yourselves and for all the flock, among which the Holy Spirit has made you overseers, to shepherd the church of God which He purchased with His own blood.

"I know that after my departure savage wolves will come in among you, not sparing the flock; and from among your own selves men will arise, speaking perverse things, to draw away the disciples after them.

"Therefore be on the alert, remembering that night and day for a period of three years I did not cease to admonish each one with tears" (Acts 20:28-31 NASB).

Paul had the nerve to admonish his people, but he was worried about the next generation of leaders. Even the words of Jesus to the seven churches in the book of Revelation carried strong rebukes because the churches allowed false brethren to gain a foothold of influence within their midst.

REFLECTION

Is hurting someone's feelings always unloving?

Steven Crosby, in his book *Silent Killers*, writes about prevailing misconceptions that typify Christian love. He said, "If one believes that "hurting someone's feelings" is categorically "unloving," he will never take the relational risks necessary to speak the truth in love and follow through with further action when appropriate. As a result, evil will dominate and prevail, often masked behind great sweetness of soul. This brand of "love" promotes peace at all cost." When leaders have a failure of nerve, they create a perfect hothouse for toxic growth.

CHAPTER 4

Lead with Vision and Experience Breakthrough

Barry Wissler

Guard Team Relationships

The single most important aspect of spiritual warfare is the proper handling of offenses. Working together can be hard because things sometimes go wrong among relationships.

"Then He said to the disciples, "It is impossible that no offenses should come, but woe to him through whom they do come! Be on your guard. If your brother sins against you, rebuke him; and if he repents, forgive him. And if he sins against you seven times in a day, and seven times in a day returns to you, saying, 'I repent,' you shall forgive him." Luke 17:1, 3-4 (NASB).

> More people are driven from the church by legalism than anything else.

It is impossible to live in this world, especially within the church, and not have opportunities for offense, which Satan uses to trap and separate us. Many moves of God in history were spoiled because of relational breakdowns. Often what offends us is not really sin as defined by the Bible. Legalism is one of the harshest atmospheres for the human spirit to survive in. More people are driven from the church by legalism than anything else. Very few people will run from love. Even if someone does sin seven times a day, we must forgive.

Perhaps the most common and powerful avenues for offenses come from jealousy. Proverbs says, "Against jealousy who can stand?" Jealousy is a very strong emotion that can overpower us if we are not guarding our heart. The hardest offenses to handle are from those we love. Only those we care about can hurt us deeply.

"If an enemy were insulting me, I could endure it; if a foe were raising himself against me, I could hide from him. But it is you, a man like myself, my companion, my close friend with whom I once enjoyed sweet fellowship as we walked with the throng at the house of God" (Psalm 41:12-14 NASB).

In the last days Satan will use offenses among Christians for his advantage. When the disciples asked Jesus: "What will be the sign of your coming?" This is what he answered, "And then many will be offended, will betray one another, and will hate one another. And because lawlessness will abound, the love of many will grow cold" (Matthew 24:10, 12 NASB).

There is a progression as the relational strain moves from offense, to betrayal, to hatred and loss of love. Churches suffer more from destructive Christians than from any other enemy. It is important that we do not hide or deny an offense out of embarrassment. In church matters, take special precautions when accusing an elder. As we are told in 1 Timothy 5:19, "Do not receive an accusation against an elder except on the

REFLECTION
Explain God's solution for finding healing from hurt.

basis of two or three witnesses." Why? Because the enemy is always attempting to discredit and undermine trust in leaders. Since leaders are imperfect, Satan has a lot of material with which to work. We should not be quick to criticize anyone who is serving the church. As Paul says in 1 Thessalonians 5:12 (NASB), "We request of you, brethren, that you appreciate those who diligently labor among you."

It has often been said "hurt people hurt people." God's answer to finding healing from any hurt is for us to forgive and let go of the offense. A test to see if we are healed of a hurt is whether or not we pray for those who have hurt us and ask God to bless them. Those of us on a church leadership team must guard our hearts and resolve offenses quickly. We should seek to understand each other and treat each other like family, with strong loyalty that doesn't evaporate quickly.

Train for Skill

DAY 2

"For since in the wisdom of God the world through its wisdom did not come to know God, God was well-pleased through the foolishness of the message preached to save those who believe" (1 Corinthians 1:21 NASB).

Today some people carry a distain for preaching. But this is what Jesus sent His disciples out to do. He said, "Go into all the world and preach the gospel."

Confident delivery of God's Word is very critical to the advancement of the Kingdom. Loving people is good, but they still need to hear God speak. We need to learn to use the Word of God skillfully.

The Word of God is the sword of the Spirit, our main weapon. Before we run to battle we must become familiar with the use of our sword. Much practice is required to be skillful in the use of a sword. We would be fools to think we do not need training. Remember, it does not become the sword until it is drawn and delivered somewhere. Just having a Bible and reading it is not the main use of God's Word. We must use it. Declare it. Insert it carefully into situations.

> Many today have adopted an anti-intellectual bias.

The sword of the Spirit terrifies the devil. Jesus modeled what we should do during temptation when He said, "It is written." The devil runs away from the words of God with confusion and terror. It is the sword of the Lord that will defeat Leviathan the twisted serpent.

"In that day the Lord will punish Leviathan the fleeing serpent, With His fierce and great and mighty sword, Even Leviathan the twisted serpent" (Isaiah 27:1 NASB).

The Word of God is a two-edged sword which cuts both ways. By it, we both convert unbelievers and destroy our enemies with the same sword. The sword is used to both secure a kingdom and keep it from those who would take it away. As servants of the Lord, we must stand ready to use the Word at all times.

"I solemnly charge you in the presence of God and of Christ Jesus, who is to judge the living and the dead, and by His appearing and His kingdom: preach the word; be ready in season and out of season; reprove, rebuke, exhort, with great patience and instruction. For the time will come when they will not endure sound doctrine; but wanting to have their ears tickled, they will accumulate for themselves teachers in accordance to their own desires, and will turn away their ears from the truth and will turn aside to myths" (2 Timothy 4:1-4 NASB).

Leaders have authority when we exhort, instruct and rebuke using the word of God. Leaders get into trouble when they expect to have authority through voicing their own ideas and opinions. I once heard David Ireland, a friend of mine, tell leaders, "Read until you are full, think until you are clear, and pray until you are hot."

Read widely so you know how others think about scripture. Even read things you disagree with. Read widely so you know a lot about God's world. I advise: Sell your shirts and use the money to buy books. Know all about the subjects you address.

REFLECTION
Are you quick to act on your own ideas and opinions?

And, of course, think until you are clear. Many today have adopted an anti-intellectual bias. As Christians it is not acceptable for us to have full hearts and empty heads. God gave us a brain so that we can use it. As long as reason does not replace God, we can have our thoughts guided by the Spirit. So fill your life, your days and your mind with scripture.

Vision Leads to Destiny

"Where there is no vision, the people are unrestrained" (Proverbs 29:18 NASB).

Vision is what we perceive, by the Holy Spirit, pertaining to God's purpose for us. Leadership expert Aubrey Malphurs writes in *Being Leaders: The Nature of Authentic Christian Leadership*, "It is a mental picture of a preferred future that God gives us. Just as a train needs tracks to guide its way, so we need vision to guide us. This is true for each

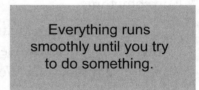

Everything runs smoothly until you try to do something.

of us as individuals but also true for organizations. We must each see how our personal vision fits within a collective corporate vision." I have heard it said, "A man without vision is a man without a future. A man without a future will always return to his past." Each of us needs a guiding vision for our lives. It's helpful to take time to discover vision and write it out to help us stay focused.

"Then the Lord answered me and said, 'Record the vision and inscribe it on tablets that the one who reads it may run. For the vision is yet for the appointed time; it hastens toward the goal, and it will not fail. Though it tarries, wait for it; for it will certainly come, it will not delay'" (Habakkuk 2:2 NASB).

Each of us has a destiny, which is the will of God for us. But it is a potential destiny because we do not reach our destiny automatically. We reach our destiny by following the vision that God gives us. When God gives us vision, it creates a spiritual momentum to move towards our destiny. Momentum results in spiritual advancement, but we must maintain our gains through spiritual warfare. Warfare always happens during forward advancement. It is a certainty. Everything runs smoothly until you try to do something.

Vision and faith go hand in hand. Faith has eyes. We see things in faith before we see them in the physical realm. On opening day of Disney World someone asked Walt Disney how it feels to see the park open. He replied that he had seen the park in his mind's eyes for years.

I have been fascinated by the tremendous vision and faith of the heroes of the Bible. Noah had tremendous long-term vision, which he followed against much opposition. He had to put up with the ridicule of others who did not understand.

Sometimes others will not understand your vision. Abraham set out not knowing exactly where he was going, but he followed a vision in his heart. We are told he was searching for a city whose builder and maker was God. He found it!

Moses was given vision for delivering a million people from slavery who had no weapons or military skill. Nehemiah had a vision to rebuild the wall of Jerusalem. But, he met continual opposition. The whole project was opposed continually, but he persevered through setbacks and ridicule until he saw in the natural what he first saw in his heart. Their destinies were shaped by their vision, but what if they hadn't followed their vision?

What if Noah had not built the ark because conventional wisdom said it was unnecessary? What if Abraham had stayed home and assumed there really was not a Promised Land? What if Moses had figured that Pharaoh's political and military machine was just too big to beat? What if Nehemiah had given in to the ridicule and opposition to the rebuilding?

Vision will take you to your destiny. You need it to gain momentum and

REFLECTION

What if Moses had figured that Pharaoh's political and military machine was just too big to beat?

advancement in your own life and in your organization. Never allow smallness of vision to rule your life. Never allow circumstances to limit your vision. Instead, let God lead you into changing your circumstances.

Vision Destroyers that Kill Vision

It seems that everything in life may go fine until you try to do something. This is especially true in kingdom work where there is spiritual opposition as we move forward. Leaders need to learn to keep vision alive in order to persevere.

Whenever we attempt to make progress in fulfilling our vision there are those who become vision destroyers. When Joshua sent the spies to access the land, they came back with very mixed reports. Many of the spies were very negative and talked about how large the inhabitants were and how the cities were fortified. All they could foresee were the problems. But Caleb who said, "We should go up and take possession of the land, for we can certainly do it." But the men who had gone up with him said, "We can't attack those people; they are stronger than we are." And they spread among the Israelites a bad report" (Numbers 13:30-31 NASB).

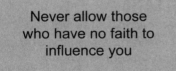

Never allow those who have no faith to influence you

The difference was simply perspective. Caleb was a visionary. But the others acted as vision destroyers. They were not only negative but also spread their negativity to others.

Some people magnify problems instead of the vision. A visionary will not allow problems or obstacles to stop their pursuit of the vision. Never allow those who have no faith to influence you! Don't let them get close to you. Sometimes everybody around you will seem discouraging, but visionary leaders must persevere like Joshua and Caleb did.

In 1840 people believed that anybody traveling more than thirty miles per hour would suffocate. Today we are glad that some believed that going faster was possible.

A powerful story about vision from the Bible is how Nehemiah rebuilt the temple. He was a great visionary who had a great start as the king gave him permission and materials. Nehemiah had others agree to rise and build when he shared the vision with them. But a few men mocked him and despised the rebuilders. Ridicule is very powerful. The mockers also accused Nehemiah of wrongdoing. They betrayed Nehemiah and spoke to the wealthy men to influence them against the project. Perhaps they were jealous of the progress. Jealousy is very powerful. Scripture asks who can stand against jealousy.

As the builders began to close the breaches in the wall, some became very angry and they conspired together to cause a disturbance in Jerusalem to try to stop the work. Angry people will always find each other and begin to work together. If they see they cannot stop the work, they will seek to cause confusion. Sometimes you need to ignore negative people and keep working.

REFLECTION
How should we handle vision destroyers?

These enemies of Nehemiah also called for a meeting to talk about it all. But Nehemiah had priorities that allowed him to say no to the meeting. Vision will give you the ability to say no to things that will distract you. When this did not work, the enemies tried to make

Nehemiah afraid by saying he was in danger of being killed.

Nehemiah recognized that they were trying to intimidate him and discredit his name. Every step of the way Nehemiah faced opposition aimed at discouraging him. But he was able to recognize the intent of these enemies and resist them.

Every calling from God and every task worth your effort will have discouraging opposition. You may need to listen to your critics and consider some objections and questions from others. But when you are certain that God has called you to a task, you need to push past negativity and even failure. Many who succeeded at great things in history failed repeatedly or had many obstacles to overcome. Never allow failure to set your course in life. You need to get up again and again. Never give up!

Learn from the Breakthrough Pig

DAY 5

Everyone whom God calls experiences resistance from the enemy. We engage in spiritual warfare. Typically the pattern goes something like this: God calls us but as soon as the enemy understands that we intend to obey God, the enemy comes against us. We enter into warfare because of our calling; the battle is real. But God will bring us to a place where He will give us a breakthrough if we persevere. While breakthrough will come from God, we should not be passive in the process. This is illustrated by David's struggle with the Philistines.

"When the Philistines heard that David had been anointed king over all Israel, all the Philistines went up in search of David; and David heard of it and went out against them. So they came up to Baal-perazim, and David defeated them there; and David said, 'God has broken through my enemies by my hand, like the breakthrough of waters.' Therefore they named that place Baal-perazim" (1 Chronicles 14:8-11 NASB).

So David named this site "Place of Breakthrough." Notice that as soon as David was anointed, his enemies came against him. David's reaction was not to retreat in fear but to go out against them. While there was a real battle with real struggle and loss, David defeated his enemies as God gave him the breakthrough. But notice that David said that God did this "by my hand." David was not a passive spectator but an active participant. He needed to fight and persevere in order to arrive at the breakthrough.

> We enter into warfare because of our calling, and the battle is real.

Many times, people who believe in miracles can become passive, expecting everything to fall out of the sky. While God does do wonders, he often does so with our participation. We must be willing to endure warfare; often the warfare is most intense just before the breakthrough.

Before I became a pastor, I was a farmer and raised pigs and cattle. The pigs were often let out in a pasture controlled by an electric fence. The fence did not hurt the pigs, but they did experience discomfort when they touched the thin wire that formed the boundary around the field. When we put the pigs into a new pasture, they had to find the boundaries. This meant a few days of squealing, but soon the pigs settled down peacefully, content to remain within the boundaries.

A similar scenario happens between the enemy and many believers. When we as believers begin to

REFLECTION

Do you prefer living in a comfort zone rather than breaking through barriers?

move out in a new calling or gift, we immediately come against a barrier that we need to get past. Often the discomfort that the enemy brings against us causes us to back off. We are tempted to live within a comfort zone, concluding that we are just not called or gifted to move in that direction. This is how the enemy controls many believers, by sending pain as soon as they decide to move out into new things.

There was one pig on our farm that I nicknamed "the breakthrough pig." This pig broke through the fence three to five times a day. We could not control her. She would approach the fence, put her head down and begin to squeal before she even touched the fence because she knew what was coming. Then she would charge the fence and the wire would slide over her back. In a split second, she would be free. Over and over she did this because she knew that the breakthrough was worth the little bit of pain she endured to get free.

We need to be a little bit like the breakthrough pig. Jesus endured the cross for the joy set before Him. Don't settle for a comfortable life when you can experience a breakthrough with God's help.

Wiki Ministry

The huge assignment of the Great Commission, which was given to us by God, will require mass-collaboration. I was always told, "Well, if we all just do our part, we can get the job done." However, that can produce an attitude that implies that we can simply all work individually toward the same goal and sometime, somehow, we will get the gospel to everyone. I no longer believe we have the luxury of approaching ministry like that.

We need each other. There is an exponential effectiveness we have when we collaborate together. As scripture tells us in Ecclesiastes 4:9, "Two are better than one because they have a good return for their labor."

> There is an exponential effectiveness we will have when we collaborate together.

You may be familiar with the Lenux software story where a whole operating system was built through open-sourcing and the collaboration of many programmers. Another example is Wikipedia, which grew ten times larger than *Encyclopedia Britannica* within a few years with only five full-time employees. It is still growing through mass-collaboration, with more than thirty million articles available in 287 languages.

A few year years ago, a small Toronto gold-mining company called Goldcorp was failing and in debt. The new owner had been to a conference at MIT and heard the story of the Linux operating system. He was inspired to apply the same principle to his gold mine. He rushed back to Toronto and told his head geologist, "I want to put all our data on the Internet and share it with the world. They will tell us where to find six million ounces of gold."

The precious metals industry is traditionally very secretive and competitive; data like this is not shared publicly. Goldcorp eventually launched a contest with financial rewards. Within weeks, submissions came in from around the world. The contestants identified 110 targets on the property and 50 percent of those targets were new. More than 80 percent of the new targets yielded substantial quantities of gold. In the end, the owner's open mindedness to collaboration turned the struggling company into a nine billion dollar corporation.

I believe that in Kingdom ministry, we can learn something from this trend in business. Old ministry paradigms have yielded hierarchies, which have set us all up as competitors. Many aspiring stars became amazing leaders, competing in the games of ministry. But in order to get the job done, we need to realize that we should be working together towards the same goal. The harvest belongs to God. The church belongs to God. We are all workers in His field and servants in His house. Do your attitudes show a heart for the Kingdom of God or are you really building your own domain? Are you open and free?

I grew up on a farm. All my dad's brothers also had farms. Each owned and worked on his own farm, but when harvest time came, they approached the work of bringing in the crops as a team. They began on one of the three farms where they transported all their equipment and hired help to work together to bring in the harvest. Then they moved to the other farms.

My understanding of harvest has always been that it is a team effort. The main goal in harvest is to keep the crops from spoil-

REFLECTION
Recall a time when you know that teamwork solved a problem.

ing in the field. Everything else became secondary when everyone works together without competition. We are told in Proverbs 30:27, "The locusts have no king, yet all of them go out in ranks." Even insects work together without the need for coercion because they know the value of collaboration. We should do the same.

Need for Parenting

DAY 7

In our time, God is restoring multigenerational team-work and ministry. Malachi 4:1-6 talks about "The Day of the Lord" being a time of judgment on the wicked. "But for you who fear My name, the sun of righteousness will rise with healing in its wings." Malachi tells us that the prophet Elijah will "restore the hearts of the fathers to their children and the hearts of the children to their fathers."

> Because of dysfunctional relationships and families, there are orphans of many types, but some are orphans by choice.

Ernest Hemingway was a graphic author who observed life with depressing realism. In his book, *The Capital of the World*, Hemingway portrays the heartbreaking story of a Spanish father and his rebellious teenage son, Paco. Years of heated conflict had estranged them completely and destroyed their relationship. When Paco finally ran away from home, his father Carlos launched a long search to find his son. After many months, his efforts to find Paco proved fruitless.

In a final attempt to discover where his son was, the desperate father placed a notice in the personal columns of a Madrid newspaper, hoping that Paco would see the ad and respond.

The ad read, "Dear Paco, Please meet me in front of the newspaper office at noon. All is forgiven. Love, Father."

According to Hemingway's story, the next day at noon, in front of the newspaper office, a squadron of civil guards had to be called out to disperse the eight hundred "Pacos" who showed up seeking to meet their father. Hemingway understood how many people long for their father's love.

There is a cry in both the natural and spiritual realms to be fathered. Will we answer that cry? Spiritual fathering has always been God's method of training. Moses was a spiritual father to Joshua, Elijah to Elisha, Paul to Timothy. We need both fathers and mothers. The Bible says to let the older women teach the younger. Ruth looked to Naomi. Deborah was called a mother to Israel.

I read a story from Reuters News Service that took place in the Pilanesberg National Park in South Africa. The park had no elephants, so they stocked the park with a new herd of young elephants. However the young bulls became mischievous, violent, and trashed the park. The workers tried a variety of things to change the elephants' behavior but nothing seemed to work. Eventually, they found the solution. They brought in a few older bull elephants. Within days, the problems vanished. The mere presence of the older elephants affected younger bulls. They simply needed fathers. In other words, young bull elephants just needed older bull elephants! This story illustrates what happens when God's plan for succeeding generations is disrupted.

Paul was unaware of our culture today, although apparently it hasn't changed since then. Our tendency, as

Paul tells us, is to have many teachers but not many fathers (1Corinthians 4:14-17). Because of dysfunctional relationships and families, there are orphans of many types, but some are orphans by choice. Many are "spiritual orphans" having no one to parent them in the ways of the Kingdom. Many are "relational orphans" not knowing how to sustain relationships or work effectively with others on a team. Many in ministry have never had a Paul or an Elijah to help guide them. "Spiritual gift" orphans may want to move in the supernatural but have no one to model that lifestyle for them. And "financial orphans" have never received a father's wisdom in handling money.

REFLECTION
Name some benefits of multi-generational ministry.

We do not need to accept a state of orphanhood. We can ask God to guide us to a spiritual father or mother and seek out the kind of coaching we need. Every believer should pass on to others what he or she has learned. We all have a biblical calling to impart Kingdom ways to the next generation. God wants to heal all of our hearts and draw the generations together into multi-generational ministry.

CHAPTER 5

Balance, Boundaries and Keys for Health

Lester Zimmerman

Beware of Energy Sappers

DAY 1

"'Believe in the light while you have the light, so that you may become children of light.' When he had finished speaking, Jesus left and hid himself from them." (John 12:36 NIV).

Over the years I have learned that some people will suck the life out of leaders and demand a lot of time. I am not talking about those with genuine needs, but about those who often have their own agendas and really don't want to change. These people are often not busy serving others but are busybodies and complainers. Some of the people who come across super-spiritual also fall into this category. They have great revelations of how the church should run but are not willing to get their hands dirty with the difficult needs in the body.

> They have great revelations of how the church should run but are not willing to get their hands dirty with the difficult needs in the body.

I remember one couple who had great potential. They had the gifts and insights that could have been used in our church to help others. But they got caught up in running after renewal meetings and conferences. They went from speaker to speaker collecting prophetic words about their calling and how God was going to use them to do great things. However I could not get them involved in serving within the ministries in our church. Soon our church was not good enough, and they were off to another church. Last I heard, they were still hopping from church to church and carrying their prophetic words with them.

There are also those folks who I consider abusers of leaders. They like to criticize leaders. After meeting with them, you feel violated in your spirit. I have learned not to meet with those types of people by myself and sometimes not at all. Leaders need to set boundaries to protect themselves from these people without feeling guilty. That's what Jesus did. At times, He hid from the Pharisees.

REFLECTION
Do you protect yourself from energy sappers?

I have also learned to be careful with new folks who come into the church with words of flattery about how great I am and how great this church is compared to their former church. Those that flatter the most usually will be the very ones who turn against you later. The same thing happened to Jesus. One day the people were shouting hosanna and praising Him—the next day they were yelling crucify Him.

Some people with an unhealthy need to get close to leadership have tried to become close to me by giving gifts. Be careful that you don't get ensnared and feel obligated to please them later when they come to you with their agendas. How blessed it is to have friends in the church without an agenda. They are priceless in the life of a leader. Monthly I meet with a prayer shield of prayer intercessors who simply pray and care for my family and me. What a gift they are to me.

I also encourage leaders not to run after people when they get upset and leave the church. Let them go. Try to clear up any offense on your part, but don't try to convince them to return. If they don't have the loyalty in their hearts to stay and work things out, it will be counterproductive to have them in your church. Accept resignations and trust God to provide.

You only have so much time and emotional energy. Use it wisely. Pour your energies into those who truly want help and respond positively to your leadership. Find those who want to be mentored and nurtured. Give yourself to those who are hungry and teachable. That's what Jesus did.

Balance Is the Key

DAY 2

"Do not be over righteous, neither be over wise—why destroy yourself? Do not be over wicked, and do not be a fool—why die before your time? It is good to grasp the one and not let go of the other. The man who fears God will avoid all [extremes]" (Ecclesiastes 7:16-18 NIV).

Solomon is admonishing us not to be given to extremes but to live a balanced life. The Message Translation says, "It's best to stay in touch with both sides of an issue." The word "balance" is a negative word in some circles, but I think it is a good word and an important word. Sure it can be used in a way to maintain the status quo and not rock the boat with new ideas; but in the positive sense, balance brings a healthy approach to living and ministry. The whole universe functions with balance.

The two things Satan uses effectively against Christians and the church are apathy and extremism. If he can lull us to sleep or get us off balance and into extremism, he will limit our ability and effectiveness. Someone has said that any truth taken to extreme becomes heresy. The thing that trips up most Christians is not outright deliberate sin but truths that become unbalanced in their lives.

> Someone has said that any truth taken to extreme becomes heresy.

When we eat a balanced diet, we are healthy. Similarly when we eat a balanced spiritual diet, the same is true. We all have our favorite subjects and teachers. Some of us are more Word-oriented and some more Spirit-oriented. The key is to keep these in balance. I have known too many leaders that failed in ministry because they became unbalanced in their teaching and ministry. As a young leader I got hold of a teaching that was new revelation to me. It became my favorite preaching topic, because I was convinced everyone needed the same revelation. I look back now and pity the people who had to put up with me. I needed to balance it with other truth.

The fact is each of us tends to define balance in relationship to what we have been taught. Most groups think they are spiritually balanced and think other groups are not. We need to realize that no one has an edge on truth or balance. The key to walking in balance is to understand that many scriptural truths are held in a divine tension. If you walk on a balance beam, you know that if you become too rigid, you fall off or if you lean too far to one side, you fall off. Finding truth is a lot like tuning a guitar string. When it is in proper tension or balance, it harmonizes with the rest of the strings. Like Solomon says, "it's good to grasp the one without letting go of the other."

It has been helpful for me to try to understand the two extremes of a matter. Then I usually find a sense of balance between the two. Both ends usually carry a certain amount of weight of truth, but unless balanced with the other, it will lead to extremism and exclusiveness in the body of Christ.

REFLECTION
How can we guard against extremism?

There is a certain fascination people have when hearing a teacher espousing new revelation, but many people today long for Spirit-filled teachers grounded in the Word who lead with a sense of balance. Those leaders, churches and ministries will experience longevity and produce healthy followers of Jesus.

DAY 3

Safety Nets for Leaders

"Then you will go on your way in safety, and your foot will not stumble" (Proverbs 3:23 NIV).

Sometimes in ministry I feel as if I am climbing huge scaffolding. The heights are a bit dizzying. It's fearful to look down and see what could happen if I slip. I believe it is important to build some safety nets around us in case we do slip or the scaffolding gives way. For our peace of mind and safety, we are wise to have some nets.

A safety net that I have built into my life includes some leaders to whom I have chosen to be accountable. I trust God to speak through these leaders if I need to hear a word of caution or correction. I am not beyond slipping so I need people who are watching out for me.

My wife is one of my safety nets.

A spouse can also serve as a safety net. Spouses are often good at picking up on things that could be a danger to us. My wife is one of my safety nets. She has built-in radar discerning women who might put me at risk or people who are taking advantage of me.

Boundaries in my life are another safety net I use. They keep me from slipping into dangerous areas. They are like guardrails along the road. They are not to limit my freedom but to give me true freedom, health and safety. Boundaries are commonsense, self-imposed practices that keep me from placing myself in situations that can be misconstrued by other people or make me vulnerable. For instance, I don't think it wise for me as a married pastor to go out alone for lunch with another woman other than my wife or daughters.

Listening times with God and His Word is also a safety net. I take time for God to speak to my heart about issues on His heart. Sometime I need to stop all study preparations and say, "Speak Lord for your servant is listening." At times like this God alerts me to things such as my heart motives. Hearing God helps protect and keep me from falling.

An outside appraisal also serves as a safety net in my life. It helps me recognize whether or not I am functioning in my strengths or in my weaknesses. The Apostle Paul mentions our human bent is to think of ourselves too highly. This gets us into trouble and sets us up for failure. Having an overseer conduct an evaluation of how other people view me helps me stay in reality and gives me things to work on that could trip me up in the future if ignored.

REFLECTION

How do safety nets enable us to finish well?

Another important net we sometimes overlook is planning for our financial future. This may not seem important at the time, but it is a very spiritual thing to do. Saving for our future is wise stewardship and prudent in order to have a net to fall back on when needed. We put a percentage into a retirement fund for each of our pastors and enable long-term missionaries to do the same. Meeting with a financial adviser who can help create this net is wise.

There may be other safety nets that God leads you to use. We all want to finish well and these nets help us to do so.

Grow in Character and Skill

"And David shepherded them with integrity of heart; with skillful hands he led them" (Psalm 78:72 NIV).

I love this verse. It reflects the importance of both character and skill in leadership. We need both to be successful in ministry. I'm sure we all have worked with people who lacked either skill or character, which limited their ministry. I once worked with a young man who had tremendous gifting and potential. He was well-rounded in his abilities and possessed good people skills, but he struggled with pride and the tendency to exaggerate things in order to get his own way. His lack of character was disappointing. When I tried to help him, he became defensive and always rationalized his behavior. I had another young person who lacked some of the skill and gifting needed for a certain role, but she was one of those jewels that you wish you could clone. Her heart was so pure and humble. But the fact remains, we need both character and skill. Being a nice person is not enough.

> Often we are far ahead if we use someone who has lesser gifts but has a heart of integrity and loyalty.

I had one man come to me and demand that I recognize his apostolic gift and release him to minister in our church. The problem was he had no obvious gifting. He was only going on what some prophet had told him.

There is a limit to how much we can develop our skill mix if God hasn't gifted us in an area, but there is no limit on how much we can grow in integrity, humility and the likeness of Jesus.

I encourage pastors seeking to fill a ministry spot not to compromise on character and select a person because they seem strongly gifted and anointed. Often we are far ahead if we use someone who has lesser gifts but has a heart of integrity and loyalty. Sometimes after I put someone into a position of authority, they become overbearing or selfish in demanding their own way with those they are called to serve. Some people can't seem to handle a title and position very well. One key that foretells how persons will handle authority is how they treat their spouse and close friends. If people are passive or authoritarian in their leadership style in the home, they will be that way in the church too.

How they respect and speak of those in authority is also a key. Do they tend to gather the disgruntled around them? Do they become

REFLECTION

Is it easier to grow in character or skill?

the listening ear and mouthpiece for the unnamed people who have a concern? This is a huge red flag. If a person has not learned to joyfully submit to and respect leaders over them, they will never gain the respect of those under them. Instead, they tend to abuse their authority after they are given it. True authority comes from being properly connected and submitted to authority.

Look for faithfulness in the little things. Some people are eager help. They don't wait to be asked. Nothing is beneath them. Although they appreciate recognition, they don't serve because of that or for that. These individuals make the best leaders. I observe those who walk down the hallway of the church facility and stop to pick up a piece of paper on the floor. These little things speak volumes about the potential in that person as a leader.

Importance of Accountability

"This brought Paul and Barnabas into sharp dispute and debate with them. So Paul and Barnabas were appointed, along with some other believers, to go up to Jerusalem to see the apostles and elders about this question" (Acts 15:2 NIV).

The Apostle Paul had an amazing conversion and clear personal call from God to preach and teach. Yet he submitted that call to the disciples and made himself

> I will not have anyone minister in our church that does not have clear accountability in their lives no matter how famous they are.

and his teaching accountable to them. I have come to understand that accountability is not limiting or a burden but actually freeing and protecting.

The fact is every one of us has the potential to be deceived in what we believe. To protect us, God puts us into relationships accountable to spiritual authority. No matter our title, age, position or level of anointing, we all need someone to whom we are spiritually accountable. In our church, I will not have anyone minister who does not have clear accountability in their lives no matter how famous they are.

Sometimes people say they are accountable, but I challenge them with this: If you do not have someone who has the authority to fire you, then you are not truly accountable. I recommend that it be written into the church bylaws so it is clear. We need structural accountability; however, people in accountability groups and under authority structures can still refuse to be truly accountable when it comes down to it.

This lesson was driven home to me: A leader to whom I related fell into deception but had no one to whom he was truly accountable. He maintained that he was only accountable to God and refused to listen to those who tried to speak into his life. As a result, he lost his church. Accountability is meant to protect us. I knew another man who told me God told him that he wants him to be happy and that it is OK for him to divorce his Christian wife and begin

REFLECTION
Do you view accountability as a burden or as protection?

a relationship with another woman. Because there was no accountability in this man's heart, he lived out that deception and its consequences.

We need two kinds of accountability in our lives. The first is relational accountability not based on authority structures. We need to be willing to submit to one another as fellow believers. Everyone should be able to speak into our lives irrespective of our position or theirs. They might not have authority in our life, but they can appeal to us as a brother and sister in the Lord. Sometimes the Lord has spoken clearly to me through new believers who are still struggling with their own issues. The other type of accountability is that which comes with authority structures such as our overseer. This person has the authority and responsibility to speak into our lives. If we get weird ideas or fall into moral failure, the person to whom we are accountable can remove us from ministry. Listen, if you have authority issues in your life, deal with it; otherwise, it will trip you up eventually. Sadly I have seen promising leaders and ministries get off track and collapse as a result of the inability to receive counsel.

Remember, when our heart is right, accountability becomes a freeing and blessed thing in our lives. I don't need to fear being deceived because I have people who love me and speak into my life. I listen to them because I trust them. That is freeing!

DAY 6

Leaders in Unity Release a Blessing

"Make every effort to keep the unity of the Spirit through the bond of peace" (Ephesians 4:3 NIV).

The role of elders is a governmental role that God has established in His church. This means spiritual authority is given to the team of elders to guide and protect the local church. In giving oversight to churches, I have seen that elder teams who walk in unity with the pastor and each other create a spiritual atmosphere that releases a blessing over the whole congregation.

> Unity is the welcome mat for the Holy Spirit to do his work among us.

I have come to the conclusion that the strength of a church is largely determined by the health and unity of the elder team. How the pastor respects and honors his elders and how the elders respect, honor and follow the vision of the pastor is so important. If an elder is not in unity with the overall vision of the pastor and the rest of the team, he or she should have the integrity to step down.

The Apostle Paul urges us to "Make every effort to keep the unity." The reason unity on the team is so critical is not because we merely want to have a nice time together, but for the authority released in the spirit realm. There is tremendous authority to bind and loose and cut off spiritual attacks against the body when the elders stand in unity and pray against divisive and destructive spirits (Matthew 16:19).

Several times during the life of our church, I sensed a spiritual attack forming against us. On several occasions it was from one or more divisive people trying to stir up dissention within the church. Several times it was opposition against us from outside the church. In several of these cases, I simply took the problem to the elders and said, "We have been given authority as elders of this church to cut this thing off before it can infect the congregation. Let's pray and bind this thing in Jesus' Name." In each case when we stood in unity and authority, the divisive spirit was dismantled and the congregation was protected.

Does this mean we never had to personally confront people? Of course not, but we pray first because we recognize that many times we are not fighting flesh and blood but principalities and powers that are coming against us. We need to dismantle the principalities and powers first. Sometimes we had to confront and ask a person to stop divisive behavior or leave our church.

REFLECTION
Can you discern the difference between surface unity and unity of the Holy Spirit?

Leaders, I encourage you to deal with a divisive person quickly before they infect your people. Too often I have seen leaders hesitant to deal with divisive people. When leaders finally confront the person, the damage has already infected the body and caused great harm, sometimes resulting in the loss of a whole group of people. It's better to lose a big giver or an important person, than have him or her constantly undermining your ministry.

Leaders, I encourage you to pray for the unity of your teams and congregation: Not a surface unity in which people are afraid to express disagreement, but a unity that goes deeper than differing opinions and nurtures a culture of honor toward each other. Unity is the welcome mat for the Holy Spirit to do his work among us. Unity is worth fighting for as strange as that may sound.

Women: An Overlooked Asset

"Even on my servants, both men and women, I will pour out my Spirit in those days, and they will prophesy" (Acts 2:18 NIV).

As I look at my past ministry and the church today, something stands out to me. It is the untapped resource of women and their gifts that God has given to the church. In recent years I have come to more fully appreciate the contribution women bring to the life and ministry of the church.

We see this in the business world but have been slow to incorporate women's gifts in the church. Regardless of our position concerning women's roles in leadership, we need to recognize that God has empowered and gifted them alongside of men as Joel prophesied would happen. From the beginning, before the devil messed everything up, Adam and Eve ruled together over creation with their gifts.

God blessed them and said to them, "Be fruitful and increase in number; fill the earth and subdue it. Rule over the fish of the sea and the birds of the air and over every living creature that moves on the ground" (Genesis 1:28).

Like men, women were created in God's image. Women's feminine perspective and insight bring another aspect of God's wisdom to the table. We are missing a huge blessing by not drawing more fully on women's gifts and their discernments in our ministries. I happen to believe women can serve in leadership positions alongside of men, but my point here is to encourage you to find ways in your faith tradition to draw on the God image and wisdom women carry. You will be all the richer for it.

> We are missing a huge blessing by not drawing more fully on women's gifts and their discernments in our ministries.

I believe the reason Islam and many religions of the world regulate women to subservient and often cruel lives is because Satan knows the power that will be unleashed if women are released to serve alongside men as God originally designed for them to function. Women are the greatest untapped resource in the church. I believe in these last days, we will see the gifts of women functioning alongside of men. That combination will result in a higher level of effectiveness and grace released upon the church. I see the next generation moving into this kind of partnership in greater ways than my generation has done. I bless them for this ability.

The church is still finding its way on this issue. My prayer is that we learn how to work together and honor each other for the gifts and calling God has placed on our lives. We may have different traditions, but each can find a way to untap this precious resource in more effective ways.

I have seen my wife respond in grace to the many challenges she encountered before her gifts and calling were recognized and embraced. At one time she was merely seen as the pastor's wife, but today the church recognizes her for her gifts and callings as a pastor. We are all the richer to have her and other women leading with their gifts in our church and network. We have come to understand there

REFLECTION
What do you believe the Bible teaches about women's leadership roles in the church?

is more than one way to biblically interpret some of the passages that have limited the gifts of women in the past. We still stumble over some old mindsets ingrained in us, but we are learning. We are plowing ground for the next generation to rise up and take dominion in the earth as men and women serve side by side.

CHAPTER 6

Make Tough Decisions and Strengthen Teamwork

Lester Zimmerman

DAY 1

Make Tough Decisions Without Acting Tough

"What do you prefer? Shall I come to you with a whip, or in love and with a gentle spirit?" (1 Corinthians 4:21NIV).

As a leader you need to be willing to make tough decisions that will not always be popular. If you have a high need for affirmation making the tough calls will be hard for you.

God gives leaders both the responsibility and authority to lead, which means we must be willing to make some tough decisions. After you gather the needed discernment from your team, you need to step up to the plate and lead.

> The mistake some leaders make is thinking they need to come across in a tough way to get people in line with the vision.

The mistake some leaders make is thinking they have to come across in a tough way to get people in line with the vision. But the example of a shepherd is that you lead sheep, you don't drive them with a whip. Yes, there is a place for rebuke but when it comes to leading the church or organization forward, gentleness is the key. Don't confuse gentleness or meekness with passivity or apologetic leadership.

Take time to teach your way through change instead of just imposing it. This means we need to slow down the process a bit to bring people along. We need to take time to listen without getting into endless fruitless dialogue. Then it's time for a decision.

Our church's growth plateaued when we reached about 500 in attendance. It was frustrating because it felt as if we were spinning our wheels. We had multiple pastoral staff, but something wasn't working. The people were happy, but I knew we had to make some changes or we would begin the inevitable slide backwards. The elders agreed to bring in a consultant to help us figure out our next step. The recommendation that we received proved to be one of the hardest tests of my leadership. It required a major restructuring, letting some of the pastors and staff go, and redefining each of our roles. The decision brought a lot of pain yet I knew in my heart that it was the right thing to do.

REFLECTION
Do you take time to teach your way through change instead of just imposing it.

Not everyone agreed. One elder said it couldn't be God if it caused pain to people. But a leader knows that pain is inevitable with change and growth. There is a difference between pain and actually harming people. The surgeon caused me great pain when I had an operation, but he didn't hurt me. The pain was the process I had to go through to better health. Likewise I faced the same dilemma with the church. I had to decide whether to base my leadership on keeping the peace, keeping my friends, keeping the offerings coming or obeying God and risking people becoming upset and leaving, which did happen. This was extremely hard for my wife and me. In hindsight I know we did the right thing.

The church soon began to grow, and before long we doubled in size. During this time, it was tempting to take on the tough demeanor and bulldoze things through. In retrospect, I do wish we had moved more slowly with the process. But to lead requires us to make the tough calls at times. Hopefully we can do so with gentleness.

Set Boundaries

DAY 2

"For he says: 'I removed the boundaries of nations, I plundered their treasures'" (Isaiah10:13 NIV).

One of the key areas a leader needs to pay attention to is having healthy boundaries. When personal and family boundaries are not intact, our treasures can be plundered. Because of our role as care-givers, we are easy targets for the unrealistic expectations of other people and the many demands of ministry. People exploit our loving heart and steal our strength. This leads to frustration, marriage problems, our children resenting the church, and spiritual and emotional burnout.

> You can expect some people to get angry at your boundaries.

A leader without boundaries is like a house without doors. If people come and go in our lives as they please with no consideration for our well-being and interests, our lives can be plundered. If you want to be a healthy leader, you must set boundaries.

You can expect some people to get angry at your boundaries. They want you to respond quickly to their every whim. Jesus had clear boundaries for himself. At times, He left the crowds with all their needs in order to get away for some personal time by himself or with his friends. I believe the Sabbath rest is a boundary God created for us to observe so we don't burn out. This is hard for leaders because Sunday is our biggest output and work day. Over the years I have worked hard at taking Mondays off as my Sabbath rest day.

Moses is an example of a leader who lacked boundaries and it was killing him (Exodus 18:13-18). He had office hours every day and evening of the week. When his father-in-law asked him why he was doing this, Moses said something like this: "I need to do this because the people need me. They keep asking for me and I can't say no. I'm their leader. It's expected

REFLECTION
Is your schedule "need-led" or Spirit-led?

of me." Moses was letting the demands of the people set his schedule. He was "need led" instead of "Spirit led." In essence, his father-in-law told Moses that his grueling schedule would destroy him.

Just as homeowners set physical boundary lines around their land, we need to set mental, physical, emotional and spiritual boundaries for our lives. In other words, boundaries help define what is and what is not our responsibilities. This gives freedom. Serving is not really free and healthy until we have good boundaries in place. The most basic boundary setting word is *no*.

Not everyone will like or respect our boundaries. I still get pushback at times about some of my boundaries. I have learned there are few true crises in people's lives, although they may think they are in crisis. A phone call in the middle of the night of a marriage spat is not a crisis. Their marriage problems did not develop overnight so the couple can wait for an office appointment.

We need to have boundaries in how we relate to the opposite sex. This is critical for leaders. I set boundaries on my family time and how much people can call me at home. We need personal boundaries of what movies and internet content we will watch. I set boundaries with how much time I will spend with people who drain me and with those who like to criticize the church. I have boundaries to protect the time I need to study. Set every boundary you need. You and your family will be healthier for it. You will be less stressed, too.

Plant Lots of Seed

DAY 3

"Remember this: Whoever sows sparingly will also reap sparingly, and whoever sows generously will also reap generously. Now he who supplies seed to the sower and bread for food will also supply and increase your store of seed and will enlarge the harvest of your righteousness" (2 Corinthians 9:6, 10 NIV).

Being generous by giving money has always been a challenge for me. Primarily, the reason was my lack of faith for God's provision in my life. This became a challenge for me as a leader because God was directing our church into some big ventures that required a lot of money.

God began to teach me some lessons about partnering with Him for provision. I understood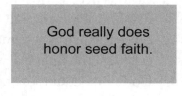

God really does honor seed faith.

the principle of tithing and as a church we tithed on what we received, but God began to teach us about sowing seed beyond our tithe.

When we first planted the church, we met in the community room of the local fire hall for several years. Eventually we were able to purchase eight acres of land, but we didn't have the money to build on it. We had a growing building fund, and we came up with a plan to plant sweet corn as a fundraiser. We were feeling pretty good about the growing fund until God challenged us to sow a financial seed for Him to bless by giving away all the money in our building fund. Plus God told us to give away all the sweet corn to local ministries. This was really hard, but our people rose up in faith and said let's obey God and trust Him to provide. I remember driving pickup loads of corn to deliver to Teen Challenge and New Life for Girls and wondering if we were crazy. I can't explain how God did it, but we were soon able to complete the building and were debt free soon after that.

This is a biblical pattern for how God provides. It is a principle of the Kingdom for individuals, businesses and churches. Over the years we have planted seed faith for various needs. Most recently we were able to purchase the neighboring farm and felt directed to build a student life center, which is our most ambitious and expensive project ever. The financial challenge seems huge for us. Again God spoke about sowing some seed faith for our provision. We have a neighboring church that borders the farmland we purchased. They had a desire to purchase some land from us. God instructed us to donate several acres to them as our seed faith. I don't know how God is going to provide, but He has already begun. On the exact week we decided to go ahead with the contract on the new building, we were able to pay off the remaining debt on the farm property.

REFLECTION
Why should the church set the example in giving?

I know the giving principle has been misused by some, but God really does honor seed faith. Leaders, I encourage you to set the example of faith for your people. Often we leaders are hesitant to talk to our people about the need for finances. But as people see the church giving and see God honoring it, they are motivated and encouraged in their giving and trusting God for their personal financial needs. Make your church a generous church. Generosity is an act of faith and worship as we put our trust in God to meet all of our needs according to the riches in Christ Jesus.

Stop Navel Gazing

DAY 4

"He said to them, 'Go into all the world and preach the good news to all creation'" (Mark 16:15 NIV).

The great challenge in church life is to keep our people and ministries from becoming internally focused on their needs, wants, and desires. In our consumer-oriented culture, people can so easily view the church as the place where their needs are met instead of the place where we partner together to reach the world for Christ.

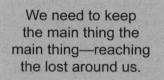

We need to keep the main thing the main thing—reaching the lost around us.

I am convinced the life and health of any church is directly related to its outreach into the community and ability to disciple new believers. New believers bring fresh air, new life and energy into the life of a church. Their "first love" passion for Jesus rubs off on us.

God said we are to go into the world—not just invite people into our buildings. Our pastoral staff was recently challenged by our lack of involvement in our community as pastors. We encourage our people to engage in the community, but we as pastors mostly sit behind our desks and run programs for Christians. We have taken on the challenge to get out into the community. The elders have agreed for each pastor to use some of their paid church time and volunteer somewhere in our community where they can build relationships with the unchurched. Some of us have become fire chaplains, police chaplains, business chaplains, high school tutors, youth center volunteers, sports coaches, Release Time workers and so forth. We are available to serve our community and not just the church folks. We set the example of the importance of the great commission. We have also asked every ministry in our church to set aside money in their budget to do some type of community outreach. As leaders we want to be externally focused and lead the way.

As a church we have done several building additions to our facilities. To keep us from becoming internally focused through these projects; we have taken a portion of the building funds and used it to build mission churches around the world. I believe strongly in global missions. We are actively supporting and sending missionaries around the globe, but we have also developed a budget and local outreach team to help us better focus on our home community.

I love great preaching and worship, powerful times of prayer, miracle services, renewal and revival movements, but too often they bring bursts of fresh air, excitement and energy without real transformation in getting the church into the community. People tend to run to the next place where they hear revival is happening. They get all blessed and happy, but too often, it fails to translate into the Great Commission of reaching the lost. I embrace revival but have learned, we can't build a church on that alone. God's purpose in revival is to equip us to fulfill the Great Commission.

I often think that in any given service God is more concerned about the seeker who may be sitting there than how great the preaching and worship is and how smoothly everything flows. We need to keep the main thing the main thing—reaching

REFLECTION
What is the purpose of revival?

the lost around us. I believe we can go deep and wide at the same time. If we lose our focus on the harvest around us, we have lost the reason for our existence to a large degree. Jesus came to seek and save the lost. He appointed us to finish the job.

Team Strength

"Brothers, choose seven men from among you who are known to be full of the Spirit and wisdom. We will turn this responsibility over to them and will give our attention to prayer and the ministry of the word" (Acts 6:3-4 NIV).

One of the things I learned early in ministry is that God's model of ministry is team ministry. Those who try to go it alone by refusing to delegate and partner will never accomplish much. God operates as a team. Husbands and

DAY 5

wives are a team. Jesus developed a team. Paul set a team of elders over every church he planted. The whole Bible speaks of teamwork.

Sometimes a leader's insecurities and need for recognition or power hinders them from delegating responsibility and the authority to go with it to other people. You will never accomplish the vision God has given you alone. You need other people's gifts, perspectives, experience and energy. A common phrase we often say at our church is "We are better together."

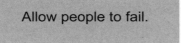

Allow people to fail.

We need to understand what we need to keep hold of and then give away as much of the ministry that we can. Train people, equip them and trust them. Hold them accountable but allow them to develop their ministry and team.

When hiring staff or assigning ministry leaders, find people who know how to build teams and are able to work with minimal supervision.

Our church would not be where it is and I would not be where I am if it were not for the teams we have in place. I rely on my elder team to help me set vision, policy and discern the tough things that come our way. I rely on my administrative team to keep thing flowing smoothly and help me with the details. I rely on my pastoral team to provide the care ministry to the people in the church. I rely on the custodial and maintenance team to keep the buildings and property functioning and looking inviting. I rely on our prayer and worship teams to provide spiritual breakthroughs and the atmosphere for God's manifest presence among us. I could go on and on about the regional teams, counseling teams, parking teams, greeter teams, usher teams, mission teams, outreach teams and many more. Our church is run by teams.

One of the things I had to come to grips with as our church grew was that I could no longer keep track of everything that is happening in the church. Sometimes it surprises people when they ask me something about our church or a ministry, and I answer, "I don't know." In delegating and releasing teams I had to give up the right to know or approve everything.

REFLECTION
How is a leader like a football coach?

The pastor or leader is much like a football coach. It is the team that wins the game, not the coach himself. The coach may get a lot of credit, but it is really the team that deserves the credit. Take time to nurture your teams by giving them resources, tools, and training. Meet regularly with your team and make sure your team meetings are not boring or disorganized. Maintain strong communication so everyone feels included and knows what is happening. Pray with and for your team. Allow people to fail. Laugh together. Find things to celebrate and do some fun things together. Your teams are your greatest asset, so take care of them and nurture them.

Vision Without Hard Work Is a Mirage

DAY 6

"In the last days, God says, 'I will pour out my Spirit on all people. Your sons and daughters will prophesy, your young men will see visions, your old men will dream dreams'" (Acts 2:17 NIV).

I am a dreamer at heart. I like to imagine what could be instead of feeling limited by circumstances around me. I like being around visionary people. Big idea people. I don't like hearing something can't be done. There is usually a way.

Older leaders have the ability to dream and draw from past experiences and pass on that wisdom; young leaders see visions of the future. The one challenge I see: It is easy to sit in a room and talk about vision, but for vision to become reality requires a lot of sacrifice and hard work. One of the things we see in business as well as the church world is that the founders poured their lives into building the successful business or church. The second generation is handed the successful work, but often does not pour the same passion into it. Within a few generations, the organization dies or loses its impact.

It's easy to be a dreamer and envision great things, but we must be willing to pay the price to see it become a reality. The fact is those who succeed work hard. They are not always looking for the easy way but for the best way. Part of the price is sweat and tears, being misunderstood, criticized, facing spiritual warfare, failure, unmet needs, and feeling alone.

As a young leader I determined not to repeat the mistakes of the previous generation who too often neglected their families to care for the business or church. I needed to find the balance. The call to the ministry affects the whole family. If one is called to leadership ministry of some form within the church, there is sacrifice and blessing for the whole family. The spouse and family need to embrace this. It can be done in a way so the family sees the rewards and not just the sacrifices. Thankfully my children grew up loving the church and still serve in the ministry in some way. Being careful how we talk about church issues in front of the children and by not putting higher expectations on our kids than we do on other kids in the church will allow our children to grow up with a sense of normalcy.

There is a price to every vision. I remember the early struggles in our church planting efforts. I was working in the hospital for a living and trying to pastor. While planting churches, we often lived on next to nothing and with

> It's easy to be a dreamer and envision great things, but we must be willing to pay the price to see it become a reality

used furniture that had been given to us. When I came home from work, I'd take care of the baby so my wife could go to work to earn some extra income. I remember early morning and late night prayer went into birthing the work. I remember the pain of losing friends who did not understand the vision. I remember loneliness, crying and travailing over the church. It took all this and more to make the vision a reality. Today we enjoy the fruit of the many who have plowed the way. The next generation will need to do the same to see their vision become a reality;

REFLECTION

Why do second-generation businesses often fail?

otherwise, the church will remain but a distant mirage or a fraction of what it could be.

We Change or We Die

DAY 7

"There is a time for everything, and a season for every activity under heaven: a time to be born and a time to die, a time to plant and a time to uproot, a time to kill and a time to heal, a time to tear down and a time to build" (Ecclesiastes 3:1-3 NIV).

Every healthy living thing that is growing is constantly going through a change process. Change is inevitable to every organization. We are either changing toward increased health or we are experiencing deteriorating change that is hindering growth. Either way your church or organization is going to change so you are wise to initiate the changes that will be helpful.

I have found that in initiating major change, you need to give a lot of lead time to the people. Begin by hinting at different things to start people thinking. I try to teach my way through big changes. Take time to lay foundations. Identify the values and principles behind the change. Make sure you answer the why questions: "Why should we go to two services, build, or do things differently?" The answer to most questions is "because people matter to God. We are called to reach more people as our number one mandate as a church."

During the life of our church, we have plateaued several times. Each time we came up against a growth barrier, we had to initiate some type of change to our leadership structure. One time it was repositioning some leaders. Some ministries outgrow the skill level of the leader. If the leader lacks the ability to grow in the needed skills, he or she needs to be repositioned or replaced. Another time it was changing the role of the elders and delegating more decision making to others. Another time it was adding some staff. I have discovered in most instances in order to break through a growth barrier, a change in leadership structure is required. Adding more programs is usually not the key initially.

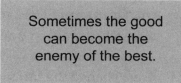

Sometimes the good can become the enemy of the best.

We also need to be willing to let go of some programs that are not as effective as before. This can be hard to do because people have invested their lives into different programs and may feel a sense of ownership. At times, leadership requires that you take the saddle off the horse before it dies an undignified death. One major change we initiated was getting rid of our traditional adult Sunday school program. We did it for practical space reasons but also because it was no longer the effective way to do adult education for our large congregation. We began talking about it far ahead of time, explained why we were doing it and then pulled the plug. Not everyone was happy, but it was a necessary change for us. Sometimes the good can become the enemy of the best.

The problem for leaders is that most of the people we lead don't like change. Most of the personality types prefer

REFLECTION
Why is change generally necessary?

the steady, normal, no change mode of life. But if you want to grow your church or ministry, you need to embrace change as normal and good. You need to be doing constant research. Things in our culture are changing rapidly. The way we did church yesterday is not as effective today. We don't change the message, but we must change the methods if we want to stay connected, relevant and effective in reaching our world for Christ.

CHAPTER 7

Fulfill Your God-given Call and Other Things I Learned

Larry Kreider

DAY 1

If Someone Can Talk You Into It, Someone Else Will Talk You Out of It

About twenty years ago, I almost quit as the senior pastor of our church. My immaturity as a leader and inability to communicate clearly the things that I felt God was showing me led to frustration. After serving as a senior pastor for twelve years, I was ready to "throw in the towel." I felt misunderstood, and I was not sure if it was worth all the hassle. I was frustrated, exhausted and overworked.

In a misguided attempt to try to please everyone, I was listening to dozens of voices giving conflicting advice and direction. I felt unable to get back on track. I was tired. Thankfully I was encouraged to take a sabbatical.

> In a misguided attempt to try to please everyone, I was listening to dozens of voices giving conflicting advice and direction.

It was during the sabbatical, spending time with God in the mountains, that I remembered the original call from God to lead this church family. The call had not changed! God had not uncalled me! I obeyed my original call from God and returned to lead our church family through a transition to decentralize into eight churches. That was the beginning of our family of churches, which has multiplied into hundreds of churches throughout the world. Today, by the grace of God, I am extremely fulfilled in my call and role of leadership.

Your God-given calling is likely to be tested. Instead of pastoring, your call may be leadership in business, education, government, community service, the church, your family, your neighborhood, the arts, entertainment, media or sports. No matter what your vocation, it is inevitable that a time will come when you doubt yourself and what God has called you to do. If you are like me, you will go through times of doubt as you struggle to find a sense of purpose in your life's work. At times, you may doubt that you even have a calling. Don't despair! Rest assured that God is in the business of equipping and calling leaders. God will not call you to something He does not give you the grace to do.

Eric Liddle, a Scottish runner who competed in the 1924 Olympics, had a calling to become a missionary, but he also had a calling to run. When he was challenged by his sister to go immediately to serve as a missionary in China rather than competing in the Paris Olympics, Eric said, "God has made me to be a missionary, aye, but he has made me fast, and when I run, I feel God's pleasure" (From the movie, Chariots of Fire). He knew God had called him to run at that particular point in time, and when Eric ran, he felt God's pleasure. What do you do that makes you feel God's pleasure?

REFLECTION

Why is it important to know God, rather than man, has called you?

As a leader, you must know you are called by God. Then you can say, along with Paul, the apostle, "I am chosen by the will of God" (1 Corinthians 1:1) and "not appointed by any group of people or any human authority, but by Jesus Christ himself" (Galatians 1:1). If someone can talk you into a leadership role, someone else will talk you out of it. You must know that God has called you.

Paul knew he was called by God to be an apostle. That is why he did not seek to win the approval of men. "Obviously, I'm not trying to win the approval of people, but of God. If pleasing people were my goal, I would not be Christ's servant" (Galatians 1:10). Paul was secure in his calling. He encouraged others to know their individual callings as they lived lives of purpose and destiny. "Be sure to carry out the ministry the Lord gave you" (Colossians 4:17).

DAY 2

Handling Criticism

Few people appreciate being criticized or falsely accused. I was once told there are two types of ministry before the throne of God: Jesus' ministry of intercession (Romans 8:34) and Satan's ministry of accusation (Revelation 12:10). These same two "ministries" can be found in the church. As leaders, we must extend Jesus' ministry of intercession to others. If we are criticized or falsely accused, we must extend forgiveness. Truth will triumph. We do not need to defend ourselves. Instead, we should focus on the Lord and His presence in our lives. He will vindicate.

Effective leaders learn to accept constructive criticism. We need others to help us see our way past our flaws. Too many Christian leaders become cynical and sour from the challenges of leadership. The criticisms and obstacles they face as leaders make them bitter instead of better! They start to feel defensive and undervalued.

In his book *Axiom*, Bill Hybels talks of looking for the nugget of truth found within unhealthy and unfounded criticism we receive as leaders. It has been my experience that even when criticism is clearly loaded with false charges and nonsense, it frequently contains an underlying element of truth. I have three choices: I can disregard and throw out the entire criticism and never think of it again. I can dwell on it, rehash it and mentally defend myself time and time again. During this process I will mull over all of the reasons why the critic is an unwise and mean-spirited person. Or, I can examine the criticism to discover the one to five percent truth contained in the criticism and use it as an impetus for change and improvement. In this way, I can quickly discard the false part of the criticism and refuse to allow it to tear me down. I believe the third response is the wisest as God develops His character within me.

> Too many Christian leaders become cynical and sour from the challenges of leadership.

When we receive correction or criticism, whether constructive or not, we must look to the cross. When we look at the cross, we look into the heart of God. We see our own need for cleansing and forgiveness and realize that although we may feel rejected by others, God will never reject us.

Although I wish it were not true, criticism and conflict are often inevitable. I read a story about a church deacon who pulled out a gun and shot another deacon during a church leadership meeting. Obviously this is an extreme example, but the truth is that conflict and accusation does happen in churches. Conflicts may leave individuals feeling hurt, ignored, confused, isolated or threatened. As shepherds we need to lovingly confront those who cause division in our churches.

REFLECTION
What is the secret for enabling obstacles to make us better, not bitter?

When I pastored our first church, one of the men in the church began to sow seeds of discontent. He expressed his opinions about how he differed with some decisions that church leadership was making. People were confused. This man's actions were also causing a strain on our relationship. When I realized what was happening, I faced my fears of confrontation and sat down with this brother. I told him what I was seeing. He received my admonition, and our relationship was restored.

The founder of Operation Mobilization, George Verwer, gives this sound advice to leaders dealing with criticism and accusations in the church, "Get more familiar with the pain, and don't let it be such a big deal." All leaders at times will experience the pain of criticism and false accusations, but let us remember that this is simply par for our life's course in leadership.

Know Your Fields of Ministry

DAY 3

I have found that a scriptural understanding of "fields of ministry" is essential for successful leadership. 2 Corinthians 10:13 states, "We, however will not boast beyond measure, but within the limits of the sphere which God appointed us—a sphere which especially includes you." The Greek word for "field" in the New Testament is "metron." It means a measure or sphere of activity that defines the limits of one's power and influence.

Ephesians 4:7 (NIV) translates metron differently: "But to each one of us grace has been given as Christ apportioned it." Here the word

The enemy can bring havoc when fields of ministry are violated.

apportioned is a translation of the same word "metron." It infers that for each metron or field of ministry, a special grace is given with it. A simple definition of grace is "the enabling power to do what God has called us to do." This is really good news! If you are the lead pastor of a local church or the leader of a ministry or business, God has given you authority and grace to lead in your field. Your family is also your field. You have spiritual authority in prayer for your field.

When I was a farm boy, I would never think of plowing my neighbor's field without his approval. The field belonged to him. By law, I could not do anything in his field unless he asked me. The same truth applies to spiritual fields. Sometimes people claiming to be God's spokesman come into spiritual fields of churches and "prophesy" things that are inappropriate. The enemy can bring havoc when fields of ministry are violated.

God wants us to be secure in providing leadership within the field he has given us. He wants us to stay out of other people's fields unless we are invited. The three co-authors of this book are my friends. I have ministered in each of their churches. But in every case, I knew clearly I was in their field of ministry and under their authority. I was there to help them.

REFLECTION

Why is it necessary to protect our field of ministry?

Some years ago when I served as senior pastor, a man from another nation claiming to be a prophet asked to minister at our church. When we could not make the date he designated work with our schedule, the man pronounced a curse on me and on our church because we had not "obeyed the prophet." Our leadership team met and broke the curse in Jesus' name because we know Jesus loves his church—He does not curse it. Later, we learned this man's ministry had been splitting churches in his nation before he came to America. We were so grateful we knew our church was the field God had given to us and used the God-given authority we had for our field.

Sometimes leaders out of insecurity give their fields to another who usurps their authority for their God-given field. Adam and Eve surrendered their "field" to Satan. In Genesis 1:26 God gave Adam and Eve authority over the whole world, but Satan came into Adam and Eve's field, and they surrendered their authority to him. Not everyone who comes into our field is from the Lord. Do not stand for the enemy interfering in your field. Resist the enemy in Jesus' name!

Fields of ministry make us fruitful within those areas. Psalm 16:5-6 (NIV) teaches us: "Lord, you have assigned me my portion and my cup: you have made my lot secure. The boundary lines have fallen for me in pleasant places; surely I have a delightful inheritance." Boundary lines don't limit us, but allow us to be fruitful in our field.

Psalm 75:6-7 (NIV) states, "No one from the east or the west or from the desert can exalt a man. But it is God who judges: He brings one down, he exalts another." Advancement comes from the Lord. If we humble ourselves, God will exalt us.

Biblical Decision-making

DAY 4

One of the most important leadership truths I have learned is to teach people how to make decisions biblically. Sometimes those who serve with us have been trained through past church experiences to make decisions in non-biblical ways. This can cause conflict and deadlock in decision-making. True biblical decision-making will honor the Lord, honor the leader's vision, and honor the team of leaders and the congregation. It took me more than a dozen years in leadership to learn this important truth.

> Avoid "the rule of the negative."

In Acts chapter 15 the early church was in crisis. The leaders of the New Testament church came together in Jerusalem because leaders from Antioch were feeling pressured by some Jerusalem leaders to require circumcision for Gentile believers. The apostles and elders needed clear, decisive direction from the Lord. Here we find three principles for biblical decision-making.

1. God calls and anoints someone to lead. God speaks through this leader.

Moses asked the Lord to appoint a man over the congregation (Numbers 27:16). God called Joshua. God calls someone on every team to be the "primary vision carrier." In church organization structures, this form of leadership is often referred to as Episcopal Church government. God speaks through his chosen leader. James served in this way in Jerusalem (Acts 21:18). However, if we only use Episcopal type decision-making, the leader may become autocratic.

2. God also calls a team to walk together and speaks through them.

Many New Testament examples speak of teams. Acts 16:4 speaks of apostles and elders in plural. In 1Peter 5:1, the term "elders" is used. God speaking through a team is often referred to as Presbyterian Church government. God speaks to and through a team. However, if we only use Presbyterian type decision-making, the team may take forever to make a decision.

3. God also speaks through His people in the local church.

In Acts 6:1-7, the people chose seven deacons. Then the apostles appointed them. Wise leaders will listen to what God says through His people before making a decision that affects them. This makes people feel valued. God speaking through the congregation is often referred to as Congregational Church government. However, if we only use congregational type decision-making, it can quickly become political.

REFLECTION

What should be done when a decision must be made but the team does not reach unanimous agreement?

Biblical decision-making includes honoring each of these three principles. The early church fathers in Acts 15 valued the church by meeting with them first and testifying of God's work in Antioch, and then the apostles and elders met. Then James, the senior leader in Jerusalem, gave the verdict after listening to the team and discerning what the Lord was saying through them (Acts 15:13-21). The leadership team then confirmed his decision.

On a team, the leaders submit to one another, but the team leader discerns what the Lord is saying through the team. When a plane is in flight, the pilots and flight attendants work together as a team. But during takeoff, landing and crisis, the captain makes the final decisions. Wise team leaders discern what the Lord is speaking through each of the team members. The team affirms his decision. The Bible says, "We know in part and we prophesy in part" (1 Corinthians 13:9). Together we have the mind of Christ.

Leadership teams are built on trust, and should be built slowly. Allow time for trust to be built. Biblical decision-making combines the strengths of the three types of church government—Episcopal, Presbyterian and Congregational—and minimizes the weaknesses. Outside spiritual fathers can serve local church leaders as an outside court of appeal in case there are unresolved conflicts.

Although it is best to reach complete agreement on every decision, we cannot be bound by a requirement of unanimous agreement. Avoid "the rule of the negative."

That is, under unanimous agreement, the negative would carry the decision. If a decision must be made but there is not complete consensus, the team leader must make the decision in light of the input from each team member.

Finish Well: Commit to Integrity

DAY 5

Three young ministers of the gospel were bursting onto the ministry scene in the late 1940s. Two of the three had already achieved notable influence. Chuck Templeton and Bron Clifford were preaching dynamos. One university president, after hearing Templeton preach to a crowd of several thousand, called him the most talented and gifted young preacher in the United States. Bron Clifford was also believed to be someone who would greatly impact the church world. Both Templeton and Clifford started out strong.

> Most of the leaders in the Bible did not finish well.

But by 1950, Templeton left the ministry in pursuit of a career as a radio and television commentator. He eventually said that he no longer believed in orthodox Christianity.

Clifford's story is nothing short of tragic. By 1954, he had left his wife and two children. Alcohol was the vice that destroyed his life. Only nine years after being the most sought-after preacher in the United States, Clifford was found dead in a sleazy motel room.

The third evangelist is Billy Graham. While Templeton and Clifford were enjoying success, Graham was establishing boundaries within his personal life and ministry. He has been a leader who has led with integrity for more than 60 years. LaVerne and I visited the Billy Graham Library in Charlotte recently, and we were both deeply inspired by Billy's life of obedience and integrity. He is finishing well.

A leader who "has integrity" is honest, and has clear and uncompromised values and clarity about what is right and wrong. Integrity comes from the same Latin root as "integer." You may remember integers from math—whole numbers. Integrity means whole or complete. A leader who leads with integrity is leading completely and will finish well. Titus 2:7 tells us: "Let everything you do reflect the integrity and seriousness of your teaching." Integrity means there is a complete openness about our lives, hiding nothing.

REFLECTION
What are the three temptations that keep many leaders from finishing well?

Most of the leaders in the Bible did not finish well. This should put the fear of God in us.

Three major temptations lurk, waiting to derail our ministry and integrity before God. 1 John 2:16 lists these three temptations as sexual temptation (the cravings of sinful man), the love of money (the lust of the eyes), and pride (the boasting of what he has and does). These three temptations are twisted versions of legitimate and wonderful gifts God wants to give us.

Sex, within its perimeters of marriage, is a wonderful gift. But the emphasis of sex outside of marriage in today's sex-saturated society makes it a challenge for many leaders to stay morally pure. As a young leader I learned that Billy Graham set a standard in this area; I choose to follow his example. He would not spend time alone with a woman other than his wife or daughters. He has been committed to "abstaining from every appearance of evil." Billy is finishing well.

God blesses us with money to advance His kingdom here on earth and provide for our needs. On the other hand, the love of money turns some away from serving the Lord faithfully. Billy Graham had an open-book policy regarding ministry finances; our ministry team has done the same.

If we trust in our accomplishments, it leads to pride. May we never forget from where we have come. I continue to tell people when I travel and speak that I am a former chicken farmer who has been blessed by the grace of God. Billy's team told him they will keep him humble. Our team does the same for each other.

Proverbs 2:7 says we will be protected by our integrity because the Lord will be "a shield to those who walk with integrity."

Join the Revolution

DAY 6

Paul told the Corinthian church they had many teachers, but not many fathers (1 Corinthians 4:15). After almost 2,000 years the need remains the same; there is a desperate need for spiritual fathers and mothers. Paul told the believers in Corinth that he was their spiritual father. Malachi tells us that before the Lord returns He will turn the hearts of the fathers to the children and the hearts of the children to the fathers (Malachi 4:5-6). I believe this prophecy applies to both natural and spiritual fathers.

> In ten years, by discipling only one person each year who is also discipling one person, you will have been responsible to disciple directly or indirectly more than 1,000 people!

Two thousand years ago Jesus took twelve men and trained them to take his place. Next to giving His life as a sacrifice on the cross for our freedom, I am convinced mentoring His disciples was the most important thing He did during his time on earth. I believe Jesus started a revolution: a mentoring revolution focused on spiritual training of the next generation. Paul followed Jesus' example when he discipled Timothy, Titus and Silas.

The sad truth is this: the mentoring concept has been only sporadically picked up by faithful believers in Christ throughout the past 2,000 years. Spiritual fathering and mothering has been left mostly undone.

Now is the time for each of us to pick up the responsibility of making disciples in order to continue the revolution started by Jesus Christ.

Jesus disciples were young. In fact, John, was believed to be only 17 years of age, the youngest of The Twelve. He was Jesus' closest disciple. Although Peter, James and John were part of Jesus' inner circle, Jesus also spent lots of time with the remaining disciples. Jesus' style of disciple-making has been all but lost in many parts of the body of Christ today. Yet through this simple concept, Jesus reproduced Himself in His followers to start a revolution. Call it what you want—mentoring, discipling, coaching or spiritual fathering or mothering—it is all basically the same thing— caring about the spiritual growth of another believer.

Paul really grasped this truth of disciple-making when he told Timothy, "You then, my son, be strong in the grace that is in Christ Jesus. And the things you have heard me say in the presence of many witnesses entrust to reliable men who will also be qualified to teach others" (2 Timothy 2:1-2). Paul exhorted Timothy, who was his disciple, to find another disciple who would disciple another.

It is our turn to lead the way and continue the revolution. Here is my question for you: Who is the "disciple" who you are mentoring after the pattern of Jesus and Paul the apostle?

I want to issue you a challenge that has the potential to revolutionize the world. This challenge is for every believer, not just pastors and missionaries. We are ALL called to make disciples according to Matthew 28:19-20. I challenge you to ask God for just one reproducing disciple (a person willing to mentor someone else down the road). Just one! Sure, if you want to disciple more, go for it as God gives you the grace. But start with one, and encourage your "disciple" to disciple someone else next year. It might be someone at work, a family member, an acquaintance from church, a friend or a person who is lonely. Pray and ask someone to meet with you every few weeks (maybe for coffee or tea) to talk about your walk with Jesus. Pray for them daily!

Every year, the pattern repeats as you each find another person to disciple who is also a reproducing disciple. In ten years, by discipling only one person each year who is also discipling one person, you will have been responsible to disciple directly or indirectly more than 1,000 people! You will have joined Jesus' mentoring revolution, which becomes exponential!

After twenty years, mentoring only one disciple each year, guess how many disciples you will be responsible for? More than one million! That's right—more than

REFLECTION
Do you understand exponential growth and how you can be a part of it?

one million. Do the math if you do not believe me. After 30 years, the number jumps to more than one billion! No wonder the enemy has been hiding this truth from God's people and keeping us busy in activity—even religious activity. Now for the naysayers and doubters who are saying, "But we do not live in a perfect world. What if it breaks down?" My response is simple: I will take a half million disciples if it breaks down. I'd even rather have a few new believers than none at all.

I have been blessed to be making disciples for over forty years. I have stumbled many times, but it has been worth it all. This is my one-person challenge for you as you approach this next season of your life: Ask God to help you find your "Timothy." Take a step of faith and help them grow in Christ.

Mentoring is not hard. It does not require understanding rocket science! You can change the world, one person at a time! As leaders, let's lead the way and continue the revolution started by Jesus!

Priorities

DAY 7

I was a young twenty-something youth leader hungry to obey the Lord. My wife LaVerne's father was a Mennonite pastor who often hosted pastors in his home when they came to speak at his church. I loved sitting with these men of God and asking them questions about the Lord and leadership.

One weekend LaVerne's father hosted a Mennonite denominational leader who had accomplished much for

God's kingdom. I eagerly asked the leader what had been the most outstanding thing he had learned after years of ministry and leadership. He looked me in the eye and said, "The things I have done in ministry are nothing compared to my daily walk with Jesus. I just want to stay close to Jesus." Those words made a lifetime impression on me.

If we want the Lord to speak to us and guide us, our hearts cannot be filled with desires that rise above our love for Jesus. Our love relationship with Jesus is top priority. 1 John 5:21 tells us to "stay away from idols" and Ezekiel 14:3 speaks of those who "have idols in their hearts." Idols in our hearts are those things we seek for joy and significance. John Calvin once said, "Our hearts are idol factories."

> Eventually, it dawned on me that we were exalting our vision above Jesus.

In the early 1980s, our new church began with much excitement. Pouring all of our energies into this new work, we discussed, thought and dreamed about "our vision." Eventually, it dawned on me that we were exalting our vision above Jesus. I was so convicted by the Lord when I read in 1 John 5:21 that we are to "keep ourselves from idols." Jesus shares His glory with none other, not even a good vision! I repented for exalting our vision above Jesus. Although our leadership team continues to believe that having a clear vision is a successful strategy for church growth, we also recognize that we can never allow a vision, no matter how good it is, to take the place of Christ's preeminence.

When I was a young pastor, my wife LaVerne and I hosted a guest speaker, Paul Johansson, who had served as the president of Elim Bible College in Lima, New York. He had spent years as a missionary to Africa and was a revered Christian leader. My wife and I felt honored to have him stay with us and spend time with the leaders of our new church. After our time together was almost over, I asked Paul for any advice that he may have for me. I will never forget his response. "You do not need to die for the church," he said. "Jesus died for the church." Then he added, "Your responsibility is to die for your wife."

I have never forgotten the leader's wise advice. 1 Timothy 5:8 tells us "those who won't care for their relatives, especially those in their own household, have denied the true faith. Such people are worse than unbelievers."

Our spouses and families are precious gifts from the Father and need to be a priority. I have learned that the Lord and my walk with Him is top priority. Then it is my relationship with my wife LaVerne. Since I am often gone on international ministry trips, I often plan a year

REFLECTION
Explain how vision can take preeminence over Christ.

in advance for date nights and weekends away with my wife—she is priority. I tell her she is my first disciple, and I mean it.

In retrospect, I realize that I focused too much time on ministry and not enough time on our four children while they were growing up. I regret my absence while they dealt with the pressures of being pastor's kids. I asked my children for forgiveness, and they graciously forgave me. God is redemptive. Our four children are amazing and so gracious toward us.

When life on earth is finished, all that counts for eternity is our relationship with God. How we influenced family members and those whom the Lord brought into our life also has eternal consequence. Knowing this helps keep our priorities in perspective.

CHAPTER 8

Scaffolding, Bricks and Leadership Foundations

Larry Kreider

DAY 1

Lengtheners and Strengtheners

"Enlarge the place of your tent, stretch your tent curtains wide, do not hold back; lengthen your cords, strengthen your stakes. For you will spread out to the right and to the left; your descendants will dispossess nations and settle in their desolate cities" (Isaiah 54:2-3 NIV).

I have learned that there are two types of leaders: lengtheners and strengtheners. Lengtheners are like pioneers and strengtheners are like settlers. They both have leadership gifts, but they are wired completely different.

God tells us in Isaiah 54 that we must prepare for the growth He is bringing. We must both lengthen our cords to expand and strengthen our stakes to get a deeper foundation.

> I used to think everyone thought like me.
> I was wrong!

I used to think everyone thought like me. I was wrong! I am a lengthener, but have discovered that most leaders are strengtheners. I am convinced there are at least two strengtheners for every lengthener.

Lengtheners are always thinking about growth. They love to see people come to Christ and be added to the church. Many lengtheners have a passion to see new churches planted. They often think globally, especially about missions.

Strengtheners on the other hand love to help people grow spiritually, and desire to see people find healing in their lives, marriages and families. Strengtheners love to help believers grow in the Word of God.

Tension can arise between these two leadership gifts unless we understand each another. Let me explain the conflict. Strengtheners have confided that they sometimes dread going to meetings led by lengtheners. They feel pushed. Likewise lengtheners sometimes feel bored and unmotivated when they are in meetings led by strengtheners.

The Bible contains many examples of lengtheners and strengtheners. Paul was a lengthener and Barnabas was a strengthener. Barnabas believed giving Mark a second chance was more important than Paul's missionary program; consequently, Barnabas and Paul split (Acts 15).

Peter was a lengthener. God used him to open the door to the Gentiles when he went to Cornelius' house. Timothy seemed be a strengthener who served on Paul's apostolic team. Silas seemed to be a lengthener when he was with Paul at Philippi—both were pressing into new territory.

REFLECTION
Explain why conflict often arises between lengtheners and strengtheners.

Apostles and evangelists are lengtheners. Pastors and teachers are strengtheners. Prophets can be both lengtheners and strengtheners, depending on what the Lord is saying through them at the moment.

Lengtheners are often visionary leaders who want to see their influence and their teams grow and expand. Strengtheners have a vision to help the team and people grow deeper spiritually and become better at what they are doing. Both are needed on a team for it to be effective. I have learned to appreciate others on the team who are different from me. I am grateful to the Lord for the many strengtheners on our team. My wife LaVerne is a strengthener who has really helped me to understand how strengtheners think.

A business example of a lengthener and strengthener is Walt Disney and his brother Roy who worked together as a team. Walt was the dreamer and Roy the practical one in their partnership. Roy did not always like the outland-ish ideas of Walt, but he loved Walt, believed in him, and worked to bring Walt's ideas to life. Walt knew he couldn't do what Roy did and Roy knew he couldn't do what Walt did. They submitted to each other's area of expertise and worked together. Walt was the lengthener and Roy was the strengthener.

If God has given you ideas for ministry, look for your "Roy." The relationship will work only if that person wants to see your ideas and you succeed. If on the other hand, God has made you a Roy, look for your "Walt." Look for someone with a vision. That person needs you desperately.

Refuse to Quit

We all go through seasons in life where we feel like quit-ting. For a season I was so discouraged after preaching on a Sunday morning that I never wanted to preach again. Then

I learned about the three seasons most church leaders and business leaders go through: the honeymoon season, the problem season and the perseverance-to-victory season.

The honeymoon season is the send off, the initial start when all is new and exciting. Then the reality of the struggles involved in ministry or business hits. This season filled with problems often brings confusion and conflict. The future is uncertain, and a leader may feel as if he has entered a danger zone. Problems he never thought possible arise and sap his energy. It is during this season that he has to make a decision to deal with these problems effectively by confronting one problem at a time. It helps to separate them, so they are manageable. Often during this season a leader feels like quitting. He can quit and abort the plan of God, or he can continue on in perseverance. Proverbs 24:10 says, "If you fail under pressure, your strength is too small." It is darkest right before dawn.

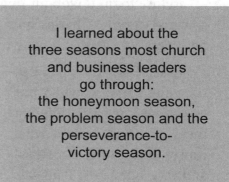

I learned about the three seasons most church and business leaders go through: the honeymoon season, the problem season and the perseverance-to-victory season.

A key posture to maintain in the perseverance stage is "not to look back." When you are driving, you keep your eyes on the road ahead—that is if you want to reach your destination intact. If you focus on what is happening behind you, you could very well end up wrapped around a telephone pole or plowed into the traffic in front of you. Focusing on past failures and problems is mostly counterproductive. It will prevent us from moving forward. We can all look back at our lives and make the comment, "If only I had done this or that in a particular situation, maybe things would be different now." If we can see that the Lord wants to use our mistakes, trials and tribulations for His glory, we will be able to move on; otherwise, we get discouraged and give up. We cannot give up. We must press through to the third season of victory.

Refuse to quit! Not quitting can be our greatest act of spiritual warfare! Charles Spurgeon once said: "With great perseverance the snail finally reached the ark."

Discipline is what keeps us going forward when our emotions scream a different message. Discipline is what causes us to "order our steps" and face our fears. Paul saw

REFLECTION
Name some focuses that can cause leaders to despair and quit.

himself as a runner in a race and pressed on toward the goal of knowing Christ. Paul said in 1 Corinthians 9:27, "I discipline my body like an athlete, training it to do what it should. Otherwise, I fear that after preaching to others I myself might be disqualified."

Sometimes during our struggles in life, we forget the message of Hebrews 12:2-4 (Message Bible), "Keep your eyes on Jesus, who both began and finished this race we're in. Study how he did it. Because he never lost sight of where he was headed—that exhilarating finish in and with God—he could put up with anything along the way: cross, shame, whatever. And now he's there, in the place of honor, right alongside God. When you find yourselves flagging in your faith, go over that story again, item by item, that long litany of hostility he plowed through. That will shoot adrenaline into your souls!"

Scaffolding and Bricks

When a new church, ministry or business begins, people are excited. They want to join the team and become a part of the new thing God is doing. But six months to a year later, some feel called to another ministry or they go back to their original place.

I recall the devastation I felt as a young pastor when the first couple left our church for another church. I was not emotionally ready to adapt to this change. Since then many people have left churches and ministries where I serve in leadership. This really bothered me until I began to understand that some people are like bricks and some are like scaffolding. Let me explain.

When you build a brick wall, you often need scaffolding on which to stand to lay the bricks properly. When the brick wall is completed, the scaffolding is no longer needed. In fact, it must be taken down and used to build another wall.

When you start a church or new ministry, some people who join will be long term and others will be short term. The long-term persons are the bricks and the short-term persons are the scaffolding. Both are needed and should be valued. This analogy has helped me so much. Now I can release people who I had hoped would work with me long term. I can bless and commission them out to help build another part of God's kingdom.

Change is hard. I often ask pastors at leaders conferences if they like change. Many give affirmative responses until I ask, "How many of you like change when someone else makes a change that affects you—and you are stuck dealing with the results?" Few people like changes with that scenario.

> I recall the devastation I felt as a young pastor when the first couple left our church for another church.

Change begins when something ends. When change occurs, people often go through a painful grieving process of denial, anger, depression and a feeling of loss as they struggle to give up the old and accept the new.

A key to a healthy transition is for leaders not to move too fast. In the Living Bible, Proverbs tells us that it is sinful and dangerous to rush into the unknown (Proverbs 19:2). We must give people time to go through changes. It is unknown territory for them. I grew up on a farm and recall driving a truckload of potatoes in from the fields.

If I traveled too fast or turned too sharply, the potatoes bounced off the truck. People will "bounce off the truck" if we make abrupt decisions during transitional times in the church and in business.

Leaders must also maintain credit in their "trust accounts." If too many changes happen too quickly, the trust can disappear. It is like keeping money in a bank account—too many withdrawals will lower the balance. It is not good policy to make major changes in the church when the "trust account" is low. Keep credit in your "trust account," remembering the process is more important than the end result.

When pastors and leaders struggle to implement change among those they lead, I remind them that sometimes it takes many years for God to get our attention to make a certain change. Let us remember this when we are encouraging others to make changes. If it took God many years to get us to be open to making a change, let's not expect those

REFLECTION

How do scaffolding and bricks relate to building the church?

we are leading to make a quick change in a month. Let's give them enough time to process this, so we can make healthy changes together.

Five Foundations of Leadership

DAY 4

I want to share with you five things I have learned about leadership that I see modeled in the life of Jesus. I call these the five foundations of leadership.

1. Security

John 13:3 says, "Jesus knew that the Father had put all things under his power, and that he had come from God and was returning to God."

We must be secure in the love and affirmation of our heavenly father (I John 3:1). The issue in many leaders' lives is that they feel insecure and consequently try to control those around them. Insecure leaders make people they lead feel insecure. When leaders are secure, the leaders and people around them are secure. Jesus led in a way that produced a culture of security.

In dealing with my personal insecurity, I have learned to look in a mirror and speak truth to myself: "I am a son of the living God. God has called me his child." Speaking the truth of God's Word brings security into my life.

2. Servanthood

John 13:4, 5 says, "so he got up from the meal, took off his outer clothing, and wrapped a towel around his waist. After that, he poured water into a basin and began to wash his disciples' feet, drying them with the towel that was wrapped around him."

All Christians are called to serve. Some have the gift of serving, but even those who do not have this spiritual gift are called to serve. In Jim Collins' book *Good to Great*, research revealed that most leaders of successful companies were found to be humble servant leaders.

3. Vision

Jesus said in John 14:12, "Very truly I tell you, whoever believes in me will do the works I have been doing, and they will do even greater things than these, because I am going to the Father."

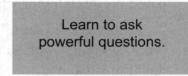

Learn to ask powerful questions.

Jesus gave his disciples a clear vision. If the vision is to be realized, it must be shared and owned by others. One person alone cannot fulfill most visions. God builds teams. Most believers and leaders find direction for their lives by embracing a vision that God has given to someone else. In the end, it matters little who received the original vision. When we embrace a vision, the vision belongs to us.

4. Teambuilding

John 17:4 tells us, "I have brought you glory on earth by finishing the work you gave me to do."

Jesus was referring to the team of disciples he had built. Jesus sent His disciples out two by two—in teams. Jesus could have accomplished His work on earth on His own, but he chose to work with a team to fulfill the task. God is a team builder.

5. Communication

In John 13: 33 Jesus said, "My children, I will be with you only a little longer. You will look for me, and just as I told the Jews, so I tell you now: Where I am going, you cannot come." Jesus was a master communicator! He prepared his disciples for what was to come.

Colossians 4:6 says, "Let your speech always be with grace, seasoned with salt, that you may know how you ought to answer each one."

What we say is important, but how we say it is just as important, if not more important. We must engage in conversations that values everyone involved in the process. How people feel is extremely important. Churches split, businesses split, marriages split because of how people feel. Often these relationships could be restored if people valued each other and showed that in conversations.

REFLECTION
What is a powerful question you could ask to help strengthen your leadership?

Jesus asked lots of questions. We should do the same. Jesus often asked his disciples and those around him powerful questions: "Who do men say that I am?" "What about you? Who do you say I am?"

Learn to ask powerful questions. A powerful question will not have a "yes" or "no" answer. Instead, it will be a question with an answer that gets in touch with what the person really feels.

Study the five leadership principles modeled by Jesus: security, servanthood, vision, teambuilding, and communication. Each one is valuable, but together they form a strong foundation for leadership.

Four Commonalities for a Healthy Team

DAY 5

"When God's people dwell in unity, He will command a blessing" (Psalm 133:1).

Let's examine the leadership principle that students who graduate from the DOVE Leadership and Ministry School tell us helps them the most in leadership: The four commonalities of teamwork, which includes vision, values, procedure and healthy relationships. When team members function as they should—with common vision, common values and common procedures—they operate from a place of security and love for each other and have a common focus so that healthy teamwork can happen. They will serve together in unity, and God will command a blessing on them.

Members on a team must have common vision to be effective. This means they must all know where they are headed and be in agreement with this direction. They must also share common values. Values are those things you believe so deeply that you would be willing to die for them.

> A leader should never feel threatened by others on the team who are more gifted.

It takes a period of time to serve with someone to see what he/she really values. When I was a young leader, a wise older Christian leader told me it can take ten years to find out if a group of leaders really share common values. I was shocked, but I found out about ten years later, that he was correct.

In addition, there must be common procedures. Common procedures are the practical methods needed to carry out the vision. Your team must be in agreement concerning how to carry out the God-given vision. This has to do with methodology and the way it is ministered. Sometimes we use the same terminology when discussing vision, values and procedure, but we are still not on the same page. The same word can mean different things to different people.

God-given, healthy relationships are needed among team members. There are many dreadful stories of leadership teams that have fractured. One church facing some ongoing relationship problems encouraged the pastor to take a vacation and generously sent him to Hawaii. While there, the pastor received a call from one of the elders who informed him that he had taken two-thirds of the congregation and started a new church. The remaining congregation was torn apart and never recovered. The breakdown in relationships had been simmering under the surface for many months. Because the issue had not been dealt with, the team was destroyed.

If any of these four areas are missing, a team will struggle to function together. Team members must feel valued and secure in the team environment. They must realize they have a job to do and are capable of doing it well. Healthy leaders will do all they can to create a team environment that encourages each member to function in his/her particular gifts. It is often good to incorporate an evaluation process when a new team is formed, so that in six or twelve months, you can review the effectiveness of the four areas.

REFLECTION

What are the four areas where a team needs to be in unity?

A leader should never feel threatened by others on the team who are more gifted in some ministry areas. The author of this little motto is unknown, but the message is loud and clear: "The best leader is the one who has sense enough to pick good people to get done what he wants done and has self-restraint enough to keep from meddling with them while they do it."

DAY 6

Trap of Unmet Expectations

I think the trap of unmet expectations is used by the enemy to cause more harm to Christian leaders than anything else of which I am aware. Unmet expectations can emotionally paralyze us.

Disappointments from unmet expectations are preventing many pastors and spiritual leaders from fulfilling their God-given destinies. When we expect God or people to do something but our expectations are not met, we can become deeply disappointed. We may have had an expectation of ourselves that we haven't fulfilled and feel helpless to do so. Or we may be disappointed with our spouse, our church, our children or another Christian leader. The list goes on and on. If those unmet expectations plant a root of bitterness deep in our hearts, it will choke out the dreams, visions and blessings that God has for us.

> This pastor, like most, had the expectation that members would be loyal, stay and support the church.

Hebrews 12:15 warns: "Look after each other so that none of you fails to receive the grace of God. Watch out that no poisonous root of bitterness grows up to trouble you, corrupting many."

The plan of the enemy is to keep us from fulfilling our destiny. Why do great leaders sometimes fall into horrible sin and make terrible decisions? In many cases, it is directly related to unmet expectations, which began with disappointment that grew into anger, hurt, helplessness, low self-esteem and other emotions planted by the enemy.

This whole process does not happen overnight, but incrementally. Compare the progression to the experience to the proverbial frog placed in the kettle of water. The frog doesn't realize when the water reaches the boiling point because the change in water temperature has been gradual, but the end result is death.

No matter what the source of our disappointment, we can release those unmet expectations and walk in freedom. The first step is to go back to the first stage of unmet expectations and admit our disappointment. If a prayer was not answered in the way we had thought it should be answered, we may need to repent of our bitterness toward God. Forgive ourselves and others who have disappointed us. If we do not forgive, we will soon experience discontentment. The grass begins looking greener on the other side of the fence. We become negative. We stop seeing the positive in our lives and in the lives of others.

REFLECTION
What often happens when people face unmet expectations?

When we enter into negativity, we are no longer sure we can trust people or we may find it much harder to trust God than in the past.

Proverbs 13:12 describes the pain of unfulfilled expectations, "Hope deferred makes the heart sick."

While ministering in Hawaii, I sat with a pastor and his wife. She blurted out, "I hate last suppers!"

"What is a last supper?" I asked. She answered, "When people in the church take us out for a meal and then tell us why they are leaving our church!"

This pastor, like most, had the expectation that members would be loyal, stay and support the church. But it does not always work that way. People will leave. If the pastor's faith remains in Christ, he can face those disappointments and won't be devastated when his expectations are not met.

Let us guard our hearts from taking an offense when personal expectations are not met. Forgive others because the Lord has forgiven us. Speak blessing to those who have hurt or disappointed us. Remember, forgiving does not mean that what the person did was right. They were probably wrong. But forgiveness releases both us and the one who has hurt us to experience the Lord's intervention.

Seasons

"To everything there is a season, and a time to every purpose under heaven" (Ecclesiastes 3:1).

As I look back on my life of leadership, I have found there have been clear seasons in my life. For me, most of the seasons have covered fifteen-year spans.

The first fifteen years of my life I was learning about life. The second fifteen-year season (ages 15-30) I was learning about leadership. During this season I was a youth leader, and LaVerne and I led a mission base for one year on an island off the coast of South Carolina. Later, I became a leader of a youth Bible study and outreach ministry in northern Lancaster County, Pennsylvania.

The third season (ages 30-45) I was the senior pastor of DOVE Christian Fellowship that had grown from 25 people to more than 2,000.

The fourth fifteen-year season (ages 45-60) I led a team to start a global church movement called DOVE International. I earned my Master's degree during this season graduating at age 60, which demonstrates that it is never too late to learn.

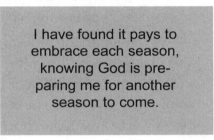

I have found it pays to embrace each season, knowing God is preparing me for another season to come.

I am now in my fifth expected fifteen-year period (ages 60-75), focusing on training a younger generation to lead DOVE International. In about ten years at age 75, I expect to move into my sixth fifteen-year season and serve as an ambassador for DOVE International, advising the team as desired and needed, writing and serving the body of Christ.

Whatever you are facing at this moment, remember, it is just for a season. Jesus lived his life in seasons. He spent his first 12 years growing up. Until he was 30 years old, Jesus helped his father in the carpenter shop. After three years of training his disciples and going to the cross for our sins, Jesus was raised from the dead. After 40 days, He ascended and is now seated by the right hand of the Father interceding for us.

Moses had seasons, Paul had seasons, Peter had seasons, and the list goes on. I have found it pays to embrace each season, knowing God is preparing me for another season to come. I am not sure why my life has been in fifteen-year seasons, but that is how it has worked out for me. God tailor-makes seasons for each of us.

As you enter different stages in your life, your calling may change. In mid-life you may feel called to a field of work that is totally different from what you are currently doing. Any sacrifices you need to make to change your career will be worth the effort because you know that God is calling you to change. I have a friend who started a realty company and was a partner in this business for many years. But he changed his career in mid-life to pursue his passion for pastoral ministry. He is now the senior pastor in my local church.

REFLECTION

How has God used a previous season in your life to prepare you for where you are today?

God wants us all to come to a place of convergence—we may try many things in life and leadership, but eventually we find our true call and fulfillment to become who we have been created to be. We may try many different things throughout life, but God uses these experiences to help us understand who we are to become. For example, I am so glad I grew up on a farm. From a human perspective, the progression from farming to pastoring may not seem related. But I learned to work hard as a young boy on the farm. That work ethic has paid off again and again in my various leadership roles.

Organizations go through seasons. Families also go through seasons. We can choose our response to each season. Learn to embrace your season. Make a decision that you will not miss the lesson in your present season. Your experiences in navigating each season of your life prepares you to lead others into trusting God no matter what happens. God bless you as you embrace your present and future seasons of life and leadership.

Appendix

Extra Leadership Nuggets from Lester Zimmerman

"Listen, my sons, to a father's instruction; pay attention and gain understanding" (Proverbs 4:1).

Several nuggets of truth that I have gleaned along the way have helped me as a leader. Not all of these thoughts are original with me. Unfortunately, I can't give credit to the authors because I don't know the sources. But I believe these are worth repeating so that others can reap wisdom.

- Choose your battles wisely. As a leader not every issue is worth arguing or debating. Use your energy for the important battles.

- Major on the majors. In other words don't argue or allow people in your church to make an issue over secondary doctrines. Most church fights are over the non-essentials of the faith.

- Leadership involves juggling a number of balls at one time. It's OK for some of these rubber balls to drop at times. They can bounce back, but your family is a glass ball that you can't afford to drop.

- Trust and honor are hard to earn but easily lost. Live a life of integrity. Be a person of your word. Be honest. Don't exaggerate. Use common sense.

- Strive for excellence not perfection. Any church of any size can be a church of excellence. Leaders set the standard.

- Finishing well has to do with how we pattern our lives now, not just the last few years of our life.

- Even a poor preacher is a great leader if he has a heart to see others succeed. Leadership at its core is about serving others and seeing people excel beyond us.

- There will always be a mixed multitude—the wheat and tares grow together. Keep the bar high and aim for the committed with your time and energy.

- Consistency builds trust. Changing your mind too often causes people to lose confidence in your leadership.

- You cannot force true reconciliation. Sometimes it takes time to ripen. Forgiveness is not the same as reconciliation.

- The senior pastor needs to stay closely connected to the worship and prayer leaders. They need to stay closely connected to the heart of the pastor to stay healthy and on track.

- God cares about the seekers in our midst. Find ways to connect with them. It's easy to be into our thing and forget about the person who has no understanding for what we are doing. Not everything needs to happen on a Sunday morning. Provide other venues for things that might not appeal to the mixed Sunday morning crowd.

- The teaching of Scripture and prayer will always be the two underpinning of the church. Pay attention to these.

- A church built on true grace is life giving and healing. Major on grace.

- The first person to speak seems right, but there is always another side in a conflict (Proverbs 18:17). Be slow to respond and make judgments on matters until you have heard the other person.

- There is a big difference between failing and being a failure. Be resilient and get up quickly. Learn from it. We all will fail at times. Get over it.

- Humility, patience and kindness are the hallmarks of a good leader—not anointing, gifts and power.

- The Holy Spirit is the key to all ministry and success. It is not by our might or power. We do well to honor and embrace the Holy Spirit's leading and presence in everything we do.

Endnotes

Chapter 3, Day 7
Edwin H. Friedman, *Failure of Nerve* (New York: Seabury Books, Church Publishing, Inc., 2007).

Chapter 3, Day 7
Steven Crosby, *Silent Killers* (Pennsylvania: Destiny Image Publishers, 2004).

Chapter 4, Day 3
Aubrey Malphurs, *Being Leaders: The Nature of Authentic Christian Leadership (Michigan, Baker Books, 2007).*

Chapter 4, Day 7
Ernest Hemingway, *The Complete Short Stories of Ernest Hemingway* (New York: Simon and Schuster Inc, 2007).

Chapter 7, Day 2
Bill Hybels, *Axiom* (Michigan: Zonderan, 2008).

Chapter 8, Day 4
Jim Collins, *Good to Great* (New York: HarperCollins Publishers, 2001).

Straight Talk To Leaders
Chapter 1 Outline
Vision, Accountability and Building Healthy Teams

1. Keep Your Eyes on the Fencepost
a. Sam's experience in plowing with mules.

b. Compare what happens when you keep your eyes focused ahead with looking elsewhere.

c. According to Proverbs 29:18, vision must be kept in focus so people do not perish.

2. Accountability and Relationship
a. Leaders need close friends according to Galatians 6:1-3.

b. Friends encourage and care for us.

c. Friends help us be strong emotionally, physically and mentally.

3. Be and Remain Teachable
a. Benefit from the counsel of others by listening rather than doing all the talking (Romans 12:3).

b. Superior attitude and tone erects walls.

c. Humble yourself.

4. Build a Strong Team
a. Visionary leaders have weaknesses and strengths.

b. Ask God to send team members who have gifts to move vision forward (1 Peter 4:10-11).

c. Be secure enough to empower team members to do their jobs well.

5. Embrace the Whole Body of Christ
   a. Exclusivity puts up walls between people.
   b. Learn from people who have strengths that are different than ours.
   c. Refuse to criticize other ministries (Mark (:38-40).
   d. Show love when others criticize your ministry.

6. Family First
   a. How do you put family before church responsibilities?
   b. Biblical reasons for putting family before ministry are based on 1 Timothy 3:4-5 and Genesis 18:19.
   c. Commitments will be tested (Sam's choice to return home from a missionary outreach in order to help his family).

7. Live and Minister Caleb's Way
   a. Compare Caleb's view with those of the other spies (Numbers 14:24).
   b. Face challenging times with faith and with feeding on God's Word.

Straight Talk To Leaders
Chapter 2 Outline

Overcoming Discouragement and Other Things I Learned

1. Swim in Your Own Lane

    a. Sam's example of imitating another preacher and the results. 2 Corinthians 10:12 warns of comparison.

    b. Importance of fulfilling the assignment God has for us (Proverbs 18:16).

2. Loyalty

    a. Importance of developing trust among team leaders (Colossians 4:7-9).

    b. Do not fear conflict. Discussions can make a team stronger.

    c. When a leader violates ministry's values, action must be taken to stop destructive forces.

3. Overcome Discouragement

    a. Pressures of working with needs of people can deposit residue on our hearts (Exodus 6:9).

    b. Time off can refresh us.

    c. Be honest with emotions, read God's Word, pray for renewed vision (Mark 9:23-24).

4. Speak Faith
    a. A leader's words can instill faith or fear, encouragement or discouragement. Example: Mark 11:22-23.
    b. When faith is tested, keep believing and speaking vision.

5. Take Care of Yourself
    a. Stress can cause burnout; the need to guard against it (Proverbs 4:23).
    b. Sam's experience with anxiety attack reveals need to restructure schedule. Mark 6:30-31 shows Jesus rested.

6. Treasure what Matters Most
    a. Treasure people, not things. Jesus demonstrated his compassion in Matthew 9:36.
    b. Spend time with hurting people to maintain sensitive heart.

7. Succession and Change
    a. Have written guidelines for succession. Moses chose his successor in Deuteronomy 34:9.
    b. For a church to grow, change is inevitable and can launch a church into future success.

**Straight Talk To Leaders
Chapter 3 Outline**

Life-long Learning and Team Dynamics

1. Become a Life-long Learner

a. Disciple comes from the Latin word for learner. The more we learn, the more effective we can be.

b. Proverbs says fools hate knowledge; wise men store up knowledge.

c. Greatest leaders in Bible continued learning: Moses, Abraham, Paul. Acts 7:22.

2. We All Are Better on a Team

a. God designed us to need others. B iblical exampes of team work: Acts 11, Acts 13, 2 Corinthians 2:12.

b. God, Jesus and Holy Spirit demonstrate working together in complementary ways.

3. Build a Functional Team

a. Character more important than gifting and skills.

b. Team members should exhibit honesty, openness, loyalty. (Philippians 2:1-7).

4. Team Meeting Protocol

a. Trust each other enough to be honest and voice opinions.

b. Group deliberation enables a team to come into alignment with united position.

c. Listen, pray, deliberate until a decision is reached that reflects God's will (Philippians 2:3,4).

5. Success Requires a Successor

    a. Transition of primary leaders requires time, planning, agreement, preparation.

    b. Outgoing leader must be secure enough to intentionally shift the emotional bond in the hearts of the people to the new leader (John 3:29-30).

6. Don't Leave Without Him

    a. Moses prevailed God for His presence, favor and ability (Exodus 33).

    b. Amazing what people can accomplish by determination. It's possible to have a seemingly great church service without God.

    c. God wants to give us grace and ability through His presence, not rely on our own strength (Zachariah 4:6).

7. Failure of Nerve

    a. Injuries in football, war and church can come from team members.

    b. Clergy killers prey on church leaders.

    c. Church is vulnerable to organizational terrorism when leaders do not have nerve to resist or are expected to be tolerant and reasonable (Acts 20:38-31).

    d. Love that promotes peace at all cost creates a perfect hothouse for toxic growth.

Straight Talk To Leaders
Chapter 4 Outline

Lead With Vision and Experience Breakthrough

1. Guard Team Relationship
   a. Learn to handle offenses according to Luke 17:3-4.

   b. Legalism is one of harshest atmospheres for the human spirit to survive.

   c. In the last days, Satan will use offenses among Christians to betray and hate. Love of many will grow cold (Matthew 24:10-12).

   d. Hurt people hurt people. God's remedy is forgiveness.

2. Train for Skill
   a. Use the Word of God skillfully (1 Corinthians 1:21).

   b. Devil is terrified by "It is written. . . ." (Isaiah 27:1).

   c. Word of God is two-edged sword that converts unbelievers and destroys enemies (2 Timothy 4:1-4).

3. Vision Leads to Destiny
   a. Discover vision and write it down (Habakkuk 2:2).

   b. Noah, Abraham Moses, Nehemiah faced setbacks and ridicule, but followed their vision.

4. Vision Destroyers that Kill Vision
   a. Joshua sent spies to assess the land. Spies returned with mixed reports.

   b. Vision destroyers spread negativity to others (Numbers 13:30-31).

    c. Visionary leaders must persevere like Nehemiah.

    d. Never allow failure to set your course in life. Get up.

5. Learn from the Breakthrough Pig

    a. Warfare is real. Enemy attacks leaders.

    b. Leaders must not be passive.

    c. David needed to fight and breakthrough in battle with Philistines (1 Chronicles 14:8-11).

    d. Christians should be like the breakthrough pig, which experienced temporary pain for the joy set before him.

6. Wiki Ministry

    a. Wikipedia grew through mass-collaboration within a few years.

    b. Harvest is team effort to keep crops from spoiling in the field. Team effort results in Ecclesiastes 4:9.

    c. Everything else is secondary in fulfilling the Great Commission.

7. Need for Parenting

    a. Ernest Hemingway's novel portrays sons who long for father's love.

    b. Cry for natural and spiritual fathering.

    c. Young bull elephants portrayed destructive behavior until placed with older elephants.

    d. Dysfunctional relationships can be changed through spiritual parenting. 1 Corinthians 4:14-17 records need of fathers.

Straight Talk To Leaders
Chapter 5 Outline

Balance, Boundaries and Keys for Health

1. Beware of Energy Sappers
    a. Set boundaries with abusers of leaders (John 12:36).

    b. Be careful not to become ensnared and obligated to people.

    c. Pour energies into those who are hungry and teachable.

2. Balance Is the Key
    a. Balance brings healthy approach to living and ministry.

    b. Apathy and extremism trips more Christians than outright sins.

    c. Be grounded in Word and lead with sense of balance (Ecclesiastes 7:16-18).

3. Safety Nets for Leaders
    a. Choose to be accountable to spouse and other ministry leaders (Proverbs 3:23).

    b. Take time to study and listen to God.

    c. Financial planning provides safety net.

4. Grow in Character and Skill
    a. Both character and skill are needed (Psalm 78:72).

    b. Do not overlook character flaws because a person is strongly gifted.

5. **Importance of Accountability**
   a. Accountability is freeing and protecting.
   b. Leaders need structural and relational accountability (Acts 15:2).

6. **Leaders in Unity Release a Blessing**
   a. Elder team guides, protects church.
   b. Team unity gives authority over destructive spirits (Matthew 16:19).
   c. Unity goes deeper than differing opinions (Ephesians 4:3).

7. **Women: An Overlooked Asset**
   a. Adam and Eve ruled together over creation. Plan continues in Acts 2:18.
   b. Women are the church's greatest untapped resource.

Straight Talk To Leaders
Chapter 6 Outline

Make Tough Decisions and Strengthen Teamwork

1. Making Tough Decisions Without Acting Tough

    a. Leaders must be willing to make tough decisions.

    b. Don't confuse gentleness or meekness with passivity or apologetic leadership (1 Corinthians 4:21).

    c. Listen before making a decision.

    d. Explain difference between pain and actually harming people.

2. Set Boundaries

    a. Healthy boundaries are needed to protect family, nations (Isaiah 10:13).

    b. Jesus, Moses, and other Bible characters show need to be Spirit led, not need led. Exodus 18:13-18.

    c. Crisis isn't always crisis.

3. Plant lots of Seed

    a. Be generous (2 Corinthians 9:6, 10).

    b. Partner with God for provision.

    c. God honors seed faith.

4. Stop Navel Gazing

    a. Health of church is related to community outreach.

    b. Purpose of revival is to equip to fulfill Great Commission (Mark 16:15).

5. Team Strength

a. Leaders' insecurities hinder delegating responsibilities.

b. Train, equip, trust team members.

c. Give up the right to know and approve everything (Acts 6:3-4).

6. Vision Without Hard Work Is a Mirage

a. Easy to talk vision, but in reality, it requires sacrifice and hard work.

b. Learn from all generations. See Acts 2:17.

7. We Change or We Die

a. Change is inevitable (Ecclesiastes 3:1-3).

b. Lay foundation for change slowly, thoroughly.

c. Don't change message but change methods to be relevant.

Straight Talk To Leaders
Chapter 7 Outline

Fulfill Your God-given Call and Other Things I Learned

1. If Someone Can Talk You into It, Someone Else Will Talk You Out of It

    a. Misguided attempt to please everyone leaves leaders frustrated, exhausted, overworked.

    b. Listen to God's voice, not conflicting voices.

    c. Know you are called by God in order to fulfill destiny (1 Corinthians 1:1; Galatians 1:10; Colossians 4:17).

2. Handling Criticism

    a. Two types of ministry before the throne: intercession (Romans 8:34) and accusation (Revelation 12:10).

    b. Criticism is par for the course in leadership.

    c. Learn, forgive, and deal with criticism.

3. Know Your Fields of Ministry

    a. God gives enabling power to lead in your field of ministry (2 Corinthians 10:13, Ephesians 4:7; Psalm 16:5-6).

    b. Use God-given authority to protect your field's boundaries. See what happens when you don't in Genesis 1:26.

4. **Biblical Decision-making**
   a. Biblical decision making honors the Lord, leader, team, congregation.
   b. Biblical decision-making combines strengths of three types of church government—Episcopal, Presbyterian, Congregational—and minimizes weaknesses. See Acts 15; Numbers 27:16; Acts 21:18; 1 Peter 5:1; Acts 6:1-7.

5. **Finish Well: Commit to Integrity**
   a. Discuss integrity that impacted the ministries of Chuck Templeton, Bron Clifford, Billy Graham.
   b. Set boundaries to finish well (Titus 2:7; 1 John 2:16; Proverbs 2:7).

6. **Join the Revolution**
   a. Jesus' mentoring revolution changed the world.
   b. Explain exponential growth that results from discipling one believer at a time. 2 Timothy 2:1-2 tells how to start.
   c. Change the world by continuing the Jesus Revolution (Matthew 28:19-20).

7. **Priorities**
   a. Stay close to Jesus.
   b. Be careful not to exalt vision above Jesus. See 1John 5:21; Ezekiel 14:3.
   c. You do not need to die for the church, Jesus already did.
   d. Family must come before church ministry (1 Timothy 5:8).

Straight Talk To Leaders
Chapter 8 Outline

Scaffolding, Bricks and Leadership Foundations

1. **Lengtheners and Strengtheners**
   a. Two types of leaders who are wired differently (Isaiah 54:2-3).
   b. Lengtheners are visionary; strengtheners' focus is spiritual growth. Both needed for successful teamwork. See tension that can develop in Acts 15.

2. **Refuse to Quit**
   a. Seasons: honeymoon, problem and perseverance to victory.
   b. Refuse to quit (Proverbs 24:10).
   c. Discipline keeps us going forward when emotions scream a different message (1 Corinthians 9:27).
   d. Keep focus on Jesus (Hebrews 12:2-4).

3. **Scaffolding and Bricks**
   a. Short-term and long-term members play different roles in church building.
   b. Change often causes grief.
   c. Fast transition cause some to "bounce off the truck." See Proverbs 19:2.

4. **Five Foundations of Leadership**
   a. Secure in Father's love (John 13:3).
   b. All called to serve. Jesus set example (John 13:4-5).
   c. Embrace vision (John 14:12).
   d. Teambuilding accomplishes task (John 17:4).
   e. Communicate with powerful questions (John 13:33).

5. **Four Commonalities for a Healthy Team**
   a. Unity in vision, values, procedures, focus commands God's blessing (Psalm 133:1).
   b. Leaders should not feel threatened by those more gifted.

6. **Trap of Unmet Expectations**
   a. Disappointment from unmet expectations is fertile ground for root of bitterness (Hebrews 12:15).
   b. Many leaders who become bitter gradually succumb to horrible sins.
   c. Faith must be in Christ, not expectations.
   d. Forgiveness releases and allows God's intervention.

7. **Seasons**
   a. God tailor-makes seasons (Ecclesiastes 3:1).
   b. God uses each season to prepare us for future responsibilities.

Reflection journaling space

Chapter 1 **Vision, Accountability and Building Healthy Teams**

Day 1 *What fencepost should you be focusing on? Has your vision become stale? Ask God for fresh inspiration.*

Day 2 *I encourage you to evaluate your life in this area. Do you have close friends you can trust and be accountable? If you are lacking in this, ask God to connect you with someone.*

Day 3 *Do you have someone you can go to when you need wisdom for life and calling? What do you do to remain softhearted and teachable?*

Day 4 *Are you a secure enough leader to share your vision with others? What keeps you from trusting others?*

Day 5 *Are you secure enough to rub shoulders with leaders who are from different groups? If not, why not?*

Day 6 *Evaluate the balance in your life when it comes to family and leadership. Make changes to nurture your children and maintain close relationships with them.*

Day 7 *Do you have a positive approach to life or are you a complainer? What steps will you take to be like Joshua and Caleb?*

Reflection journaling space

Chapter 2 **Overcoming Discouragement and Other Things I Learned**

Day 1 *Are you comparing yourself with others or are you pursuing who God made you to be? If you struggle with knowing your assignment, who can you help?*

Day 2 *Are you a loyal person? If not what is it that keeps you from trusting others?*

Day 3 *Do you have times to refuel your heart? Do you have someone with whom to share your discouragement?*

Day 4 *What do you see with the eye of faith for your ministry? What step of faith is God asking you to take?*

Day 5 *What are you doing to monitor your stress level? Do you need someone to help you evaluate your life?*

Day 6 *What are you doing to keep your heart tender-hearted toward the hurting? Are you intentionally preparing people for heaven?*

Day 7 *Are you afraid of change? If so, why and what must you do to embrace change?*

Reflection journaling space

Chapter 3 **Life-long Learning and Team Dynamics**

Day 1 *Do you have a passion to learn or have you begun to coast? How do you learn best? Have you ever had someone coach you?*

Day 2 *Do you prefer to work alone? If so, do you know why? Would you be willing to invest in teamwork if you saw the benefits?*

Day 3 *Are you a member of a team that has members with conflicting agendas? Has your attitude been to serve and help the leader and other team members?*

Day 4 *Do you and those you work with frequently have honest unfiltered discussions? Have you built trust on the team by listening to each other and moving together?*

Day 5 *How much time do you devote to training others to do what you do? If you were removed from your leadership role today, how would the organization do without you?*

Day 6 *Is the presence of God held in high honor in your life or organization? How do you cultivate and preserve a value for His presence?*

Day 7 *When have you observed or felt destructive forces at work in your organization? Have you had the nerve to confront those forces without being harsh?*

Reflection journaling space

Chapter 4 **Lead with Vision and Experience Breakthrough**

Day 1 *Has an offense or jealousy toward another caused relational strain between you and another believer? Have you been hurt by someone whom you must forgive or seek reconciliation?*

Day 2 *Have you personally received training in the study and use of scripture? How could you pursue training in how to handle scripture accurately?*

Day 3 *Do you "see" a future for yourself and your organization with the help of the Holy Spirit? Have you taken the necessary time to be sure of the vision and write it out?*

Day 4 *How well do you handle negativity from others? Can you listen but remain positive? Are you experiencing opposition now that is distracting your attention from your God-given task?*

Day 5 *When the enemy comes after you, do you respond like David did? Is there an area of your life where you are passively waiting for a breakthrough instead of partnering with God?*

Day 6 *Is your vision and task large enough that you cannot do it alone? Do you understand your strengths and weaknesses enough to collaborate with others?*

Day 7 *Have you pursued a relationship with a spiritual father or mother? Who are you fathering or mothering?*

Reflection journaling space

Chapter 5 **Balance, Boundaries and Keys for Health**

Day 1 *What drains you the most in working with people? How can you set some healthy boundaries to protect yourself and your family?*

Day 2 *What is the process by which you arrive at a sense of spiritual balance in your life and ministry? Are you able to identify extremes on doctrines and issues? Give some examples of things that need to be held in divine tension.*

Day 3 *What are some of the safety nets that you have built into your life? What nets do you believe God wants you to add for yourself and your family?*

Day 4 *How do you handle people who come to you with criticism of the church or leaders? We know what skill looks like but what does integrity look like in a leader?*

Day 5 *Who are you structurally accountable to and who has the authority to remove you if needed? Who in your life would you listen to if that person told you that you were deceived?*

Day 6 *In practical ways, how do we endeavor to keep the unity in our church or organization? What is the difference between false unity and real unity? How can we disagree and still keep the spirit of unity?*

Day 5 *What does it mean for men and women to rule and take dominion together according to God's plan in Genesis 1:28? How do you incorporate the gifts and wisdom of women in your ministry? How could you do better?*

Reflection journaling space

Chapter 6 **Make Tough Decisions and Strengthen Teamwork**

Day 1 *Having people like and affirm us is healthy, but at what point does it become unhealthy and affect our ability to lead? Is there a decision you need to make or a conversation you need to have, but you are holding back because of the fear of man?*

Day 2 *What are some boundaries you have set for yourself and why? Why do some people have trouble setting boundaries?*

Day 3 *How hard is it for you to be generous and to trust God for your financial needs? Read 1 Kings 17:7-16. What seed did the widow sow? How much faith did it require of her?*

Day 4 *How externally focused is your church or ministry? How is it actually building relationships with the un-churched? How many unchurched friends do you personally have? How do you relate to them?*

Day 5 *How well have you learned to delegate? If you are too busy, this could be an indicator. What are some keys to healthy delegating and team building?*

Day 6 *What sacrifices do you think it will take to make your vision a reality? How do we balance home life with business and church life? Do you feel you have found the balance? What would your spouse and kids say?*

Day 7 *Is change hard for you? Why or why not? Is the area of ministry you oversee as effective today as it was five to ten years ago? Could it be more effective? Why or why not? What changes might be worth considering?*

Reflection journaling space

Chapter 7 **Fulfill Your God-given Call and Other Things I Learned**

Day 1 *Do you have doubts about your call to leadership? How can you tell if you are fulfilling God's call?*

Day 2 *How do you feel you handle criticism and accusation? What is the healthiest way to respond to criticism?*

Day 3 *How do you define a field of ministry? What is a field God has given to you?*

Day 4 *Which of the three principles of leadership comes most natural for you? How can you apply this to your situation?*

Day 5 *What are some boundaries you have established in your life in order to be a person of integrity? What do you want your tombstone to say about you?*

Day 6 *Who are those who look to you as a spiritual father/mother? Who will be your next reproducing disciple (2 Timothy 2:2)?*

Day 7 *What are your top priorities? What do you worship? Should you be making any changes?*

Reflection journaling space

Chapter 8 Scaffolding, Bricks and Leadership Foundations

Day 1 *Are you primarily a lengthener or a strengthener? Do you have a team of diversity?*

Day 2 *What are the three seasons we all go through? Which season are you in right now?*

Day 3 *Can you think of persons you know who were like scaffolding? What do you need to remember about leading people through change?*

Day 4 *What are the five foundations of leadership? Which of these five foundations do you need to learn to be more effective?*

Day 5 *What are the four areas of commonality for any team to function properly? Does this apply to any teams on which you are serving or have served?*

Day 6 *Are you experiencing unmet expectations in your life and allowing a root of bitterness to grow? Do you know others who need help to be freed from a root of bitterness?*

Day 7 *What season of life are you experiencing presently? What is the Lord teaching you in this present season?*

Larry Kreider

Larry Kreider serves as International Director of DOVE International, a network of churches throughout the world. For more than three decades, DOVE has used the New Testament "house to house" strategy of building the church with small groups.

As founder of DOVE International, Larry initially served for 15 years as senior pastor of DOVE Christian Fellowship in Pennsylvania, which grew from a single cell group to more than 2,300 in 10 years. Today, DOVE believers meet in 350 congregations and in thousands of small groups in five continents of the world.

In 1971, Larry helped establish a youth ministry that targeted unchurched youth in northern Lancaster County, Pennsylvania. DOVE grew out of the ensuing need for a flexible New Testament-style church that could assist these new believers.

Larry and his wife LaVerne teach worldwide and encourage believers to reach out from house to house, city to city and nation to nation, and empower and train others to do the same.

Larry writes for Christian periodicals and has written 36 books that have sold more than 500,000 copies, with many translated into other languages. Larry earned his Masters of Ministry with a concentration on leadership from Southwestern Christian University. He and his wife have been married 44 years and live in Lititz, Pennsylvania. They enjoy spending time with their four "amazing children, two sons-in-law and the five best grandkids in the world."

Read Larry's blog at www.dcfi.org/blog
Like Larry and LaVerne Kreider on Facebook
Follow Larry Kreider on Twitter

Sam Smucker

Sam Smucker served as lead pastor of Worship Center in Lancaster, Pennsylvania for almost 40 years. After he and his wife Sherlyn graduated from Rhema Bible College in Tulsa, Oklahoma in 1977, they returned to their hometown to pioneer and pastor a new congregation—Worship Center—which has grown from 25 people to more than 3,800.

Sam oversees the Worship Center Ministers' Network, which consists of twelve churches, missionaries in foreign nations, and leaders of ministries locally and stateside. Sam is the Regional Director of the Northeast Region of Rhema Ministerial Association with its approximately 150 ministers.

Pastor Sam and his wife Sherlyn teach people to build their lives on the unshakable foundation of the Word of God and walk in victory through Jesus Christ. The Smuckers' vision is to help people find purpose in Jesus Christ through: Experiencing God, Growing Together, and Serving Our World. Sam and Sherlyn travel extensively internationally and nationally to minister in churches and teach conferences for pastors and leaders. Their heart's desire is to see leaders rise up and lead their people in the strength and power of the Holy Spirit.

Sam has written a book, *Renewing the Mind* and co-authored the book *The Fruit of the Spirit*. In addition to Rhema, Sam has studied at the Pittsburgh School of the Bible.

Sam and Sherlyn, reside in Lancaster, Pennsylvania, and have four children, five grandchildren and two great-grandchildren.

Barry Wissler

After planting and pastoring a local church for 37 years, Barry's passion for the Kingdom of God and the work of the Holy Spirit is focused on leading HarvestNet International, a network of churches and ministries. After a season of youth ministry at 17 years of age, Barry helped plant Ephrata Community Church in 1977. He soon was appointed senior pastor while he continued to farm and attend Bible school. Adopting the model of Antioch, the church experienced an out-pouring of the Holy Spirit in the late 1990s.

Under Barry's leadership, ECC planted several other congregations and formed a network of several hundred churches and ministries called HarvestNet International. HarvestNet also operates many collaborative ministries including a school of supernatural ministry and Gateway House of Prayer. In order to devote himself to leading the network and training leaders, Barry transferred church leadership to a successor in 2014. Barry's work takes him throughout the United States and to many nations.

A strong advocate for collaboration and teamwork, Barry's closest partner in ministry is his wife Cheryl, who always travels with him. They have two adult children and a daughter-in-law.

Barry holds a Bachelor of Arts in Biblical Studies from Geneva College, and a Master of Arts from Westminster Theological. He is pursuing a Doctoral Degree with the Randy Clark Scholars.

For more of Barry's writings, check out his blog at http://harvestnetinternational.com/blog

Lester Zimmerman

Lester Zimmerman and his wife Erma serve as senior pastors of Petra Church in New Holland, Pennsylvania. They founded the church more than thirty years ago and continue to see the church grow and expand its outreach locally and globally. Prior to founding Petra, the Zimmermans were involved in inner-city ministry and church planting in Baltimore, Maryland. Lester serves as lead apostle to the Hopewell Network of Churches, which includes 17 churches stateside and five international networks.

In addition, Lester serves as a police chaplain in his community. He encourages Petra Church to be externally focused in both local and global missions. The church has a strong community presence and several churches have been planted out of Petra. In addition to local missions, they have sent short-term and long-term missionaries to more than 40 countries. Lester's teachings are practical and encouraging, drawing from his life experience of growing up on a farm, mental health work, mission work and many years of hands-on ministry.

Lester describes his core values as being focused on grace, healing and the harvest with a strong dependency on the Holy Spirit. His most recent focus has been on leadership development with a heart to see the next generation of leaders equipped and released into ministry.

He has a Masters of Ministry Degree and teaches in the DOVE-Hopewell Leadership and Ministry School. He and his wife have two married daughters and two granddaughters.

For more about Petra, visit the Websites: www.petra.church and www.hopewellnetwork.org

TRAIN LEADERS AT YOUR CHURCH

Online Training for Leadership and Ministry

The DOVE-Hopewell Leadership and Ministry School has been training leaders for 20 years. More than 500 graduates are successfully engaged in the church and marketplace. The school provides practical biblical training as well as Holy Spirit-empowered impartation and activation. Students are prepared for a lifetime of leadership and ministry. Participate in nine-weekend intensives and complete the entire school.

Start a Campus: Train a group of leaders at your own church with the live webcast from our DOVE-Hopewell school in Pennsylvania. Webcasting allows groups and individual students to attend via the internet. Students send questions via text, email and the webcast chat feature also allows for discussion. Students may transfer credit to Chesapeake Bible College and Seminary.

DOVE-Hopewell Leadership and Ministry School
**For details and class schedule
visit www.dcfi.org/training**

Growing the Fruit of the Holy Spirit

Nine character qualities for healthy living help detect if your life is yielding abundant fruit? This book provides a spiritual health check. Allow the Holy Spirit to cultivate and grow the life-transforming fruit of the Spirit into your daily routine! Includes teaching outlines and questions for group study *by Larry Kreider and Sam Smucker, 160 pages* **$14.99**

Biblical Foundation Series

This series by Larry Kreider covers basic Christian doctrine. Practical illustrations accompany the easy-to-understand format. Use for small group teachings (48 outlines), in mentoring relationship or as a daily devotional. *by Larry Kreider, Each book has 64 pages:* **$4.99** each, 12 Book Set: **$39**
Available in Spanish and French.

Titles in this series:
1. **Knowing Jesus Christ as Lord**
2. **The New Way of Living**
3. **New Testament Baptisms**
4. **Building For Eternity**
5. **Living in the Grace of God**
6. **Freedom from the Curse**
7. **Learning to Fellowship with God**
8. **What is the Church?**
9. **Authority and Accountability**
10. **God's Perspective on Finances**
11. **Called to Minister**
12. **The Great Commission**

The Cry for Spiritual Mothers and Fathers

Returning to the biblical truth of spiritual parenting is necessary so believers are not left fatherless and disconnected. Learn how loving, seasoned spiritual fathers and mothers help spiritual children reach their full potential in Christ. *by Larry Kreider, 224 pages:* $14.99

Your Personal House of Prayer

Christians often struggle with their prayer lives. With the unique "house plan" developed in this book, each room corresponding to a part of the Lord's Prayer, your prayer life is destined to go from duty to joy! Includes a helpful Daily Prayer Guide. *by Larry Kreider, 192 pages:* $12.99